The Smart Canadian's Guide to Building Wealth

by
Pat Foran

John Wiley & Sons Canada, Ltd.

National Library of Canada Cataloguing in Publication Data

Foran, Pat
  The smart Canadian's guide to building wealth / Pat Foran.

Includes index.
ISBN-13 978-0-470-83664-4
ISBN-10 0-470-83664-4

  1. Finance, Personal—Canada. 2. Financial security.
I. Title.

HG179.F594 2006   332.024'01'0971   C2005-906150-2

Production Credits
Cover design: Ian Koo
Interior text design: Lesia Hnatejko

Printer: Transcontinental

John Wiley & Sons Canada, Ltd.
6045 Freemont Blvd.
Mississauga, Ontario
L5R 4J3

Printed in Canada
1 2 3 4 5 TRANS 10 09 08 07 06

table of contents

Acknowledgements

This book is dedicated to everyone who wants to try to improve their financial situation—to those who want to find the right balance between enjoying everything life has to offer and still having enough set aside to feel secure and comfortable about their future.

Thanks to my loving wife, Carole, for all her support, and to our cherished daughters, Lisa, Vanessa and Sarah. Thanks also to my parents Gordon and Helen Foran, especially my mother for her spiritual guidance. A note of appreciation to my in-laws, Hector and Anita Blanchard, for pitching in when I was working on this book and our busy household needed a hand. I also want to thank the CTV Television Network for employing me in a position that I sincerely enjoy and that allows me to help others. Thanks to the experts who have gratuitously contributed to this book and the consumers who have passed on their stories to educate us all. I hope you achieve your financial dreams.

CHAPTER 1

confronting the debt challenge

The Beatles may have said that all we need is love, but it won't heat your house or put gas in your car. We have become a consumption-driven society, buying things we don't need with money we don't have. Drowning in debt has become the new norm. We buy cars we can't afford, big screen TVs on credit cards and do expensive home renovations on lines of credit. We're not about keeping up with the Joneses but surpassing them. Well, I've got news for you—the Joneses are broke! I overheard a couple of people talking about their finances and one person said to the other, "You know, I added it up and we have about $35,000 in debt." The other person replied, "Yes, when I add up our credit card bills, car loans and line of credit at the bank, we too owe around $40,000." This, of course, is not including mortgages and all the other expenses we must continually pay out to operate in our modern society.

We are a credit crazy society. Forty years ago, debt loads were much lower in Canada, and guess what? Forty years ago, credit cards were just being introduced. That little piece of plastic is responsible for changing attitudes about debt and is one of the main reasons Canadians are in such rough financial shape today. Building wealth is possible for all of us, and it is never too late to start. To do so, though, we must take charge of our finances, reduce debt, save money and invest wisely.

In my first book, *Canadian Consumer Alert: 101 Ways to Protect Yourself and Your Money*, I wrote about how consumers must be constantly on guard to avoid scams, ripoffs and other dishonest practices in the marketplace. Along with examining financial issues, I dealt with many of the complaints I regularly receive as a consumer advocate at CTV. It is very important for consumers to be careful when signing contracts, getting a driveway paved or choosing a daycare, but in this book I want to deal with one thing: money—how to save it, how to conserve it and how to invest it. As the consumer reporter for CTV, I get to see the most cutting-edge products and services in the marketplace. A TV built into a bathroom mirror—the price $5,000. Putting greens for your backyard—$10,000. A fridge with an Internet-accessing computer screen in the door—$7,000. Would I buy any of this stuff? No way! I do find it fascinating to see the kinds of new products on the market, consumer trends and what may eventually be mass-produced so one day I can afford to buy them. I did a story on what was the best family van on the market. This particular year it was the Toyota Sienna. I later heard from a couple who took out a $45,000 loan against their home to buy one because they wanted the best van there was. Did they really need it, or would a three-year-old domestic van at one-third of the price have been good enough to shuttle their kids to hockey and make runs to the grocery store? Do we always need the best of everything? Of course we don't.

While there are many of us who have our finances in order and are prudent with the way we shop and save, about half of us are lurching from paycheque to paycheque, spending all of it as we go. There is no plan for retirement, no emergency fund for a rainy day and no savings in the savings account. This group of people has tens of thousands of dollars in what I call junk debt. Junk debt is all of the bills that have been consolidated so many times we can't even remember what the original debt was for. Too many of us are secretly hoping our numbers will come up and we'll win the lottery or inherit wealth so we can coast into our retirement with a nice big bank account. Some plan. The truth is that in our lifetimes, most of us will have more than a million dollars pass through our hands. Many of us will have several million dollars channelled through our bank accounts. What are you doing with your money? Can you find the power to harness that money and make it work for you? Or will you simply trudge along, spending it week in and week out, living from one paycheque to the next? If you think you won't get ahead, you won't. It's a self-fulfilling prophecy. Earning more is not always the answer, either. Some people will work long hours, be away from their children and stress their marriage for an extra $5,000 to $10,000 a year in overtime. The government is going to take one-half to one-third of it depending on your tax bracket, so you may be left with only $3,000 to $5,000 in after-tax dollars. Imagine if you just tried to cut back your personal spending by that amount in a year and still spend time with your kids and spouse? Spending less on a family vacation, a barbecue or a home renovation can easily save you that amount. For a family with a combined income of $100,000, saving $5,000 after tax is as good as earning $10,000 of salary or income.

I should stress as well that I don't believe people should become misers who nickel and dime friends and businesses to try to get ahead. What good is it to end up wealthy late in life if we are like Ebenezer Scrooge, huddled in a room all alone, counting our money? If the ghosts of past, present and future come to visit me, I hope I will like what I see. No, this book is to help you make wise decisions that enable you to keep more of your money instead of giving it to large corporations. Think about it. When you are loaded with debt you are giving thousands of dollars away every year to banks and creditors. Once you have amassed wealth and are free of debt you will be in a position to sponsor a child in a Third

World country; give money to a charity; buy a round of drinks; or spoil your kids, nephews and nieces rotten with a vacation. Wouldn't that be a lot more satisfying than handing over your money to some large, faceless corporation?

If you've had enough and want to get a handle on your finances, then this book is for you. It's not easy to become debt free and make the wise decisions we should be making. It's about sacrifice and discipline; it's about having a plan and sticking to it, and making sure everyone else in your household does, too.

Becoming financially self-sufficient isn't easy but it is possible for every one of us. In this book I will look at some of the most important steps necessary to build wealth and become free from the shackles of debt. We will start off with insight from Canadians who have shown it is possible to get ahead and become financially secure (and some of them downright rich). We will look at getting your finances in order, speak with experts to see if your investing strategies are on track, make sure your expenses related to shelter and transportation are not excessive and provide you with general information to help you deal with life's unexpected curveballs. I'm not just talking the talk, either. I'm walking the walk. I want to be debt free, too, so I can be financially secure in my retirement, travel the world, help my children and be charitable to worthy causes. I hope you enjoy this book and that it helps you and your family on your journey to financial peace.

CHAPTER 2

taking wisdom from successful Canadians

I have always been fascinated with quotations—those short nuggets of wisdom that can sum up, express and illuminate life, love, money and thoughts on any number of topics.

One of my favourite quotes came from someone I met as a teenager when I took a job on a farm in Lucan, Ontario. Fred Lewis is a very successful man who has amassed great wealth through land ownership and poultry production. When I asked him what he attributed his success to, he told me this one simple thing that I've never forgotten: "If you want to be successful, just make the right decisions every day."

Sounds easy enough, but it's hard to do. However, if you really *thought* about what you should and shouldn't spend money on *every day*, over time you couldn't help but be successful. For this book I wanted to find out if there were any words of wisdom that wealthy, accomplished Canadians could pass on to the rest of us about success in their lives. I asked them to think about a quote, short story or piece of advice that they could share with others that might help them be successful. Some wrote back with advice about money and others about choosing the right career, while still others spoke of the importance of giving back to the community once they became successful. All of the comments are interesting and informative and I thank everyone for taking part.

Not everyone I contacted was interested in providing a quote, but in true Canadian fashion they were polite as they declined. Representatives for Celine Dion said she was too busy singing in Las Vegas (and I'm sure she was). Keanu Reeves was on some far-flung movie set, but his assistant assured me he was honoured to be asked. Movie director James Cameron was underwater in a submarine somewhere, but passed along his best wishes. The rep for Paul Shaffer of *The Late Show with David Letterman* said contractually Paul wasn't allowed to, but that he was pleased he was included in any list of successful Canadians. I never did hear back from Prime Minister Paul Martin, but with the kind of year he's been having that was to be expected.

Something also happened that caught me by surprise. I wrote a letter to one well-known, successful Canadian whom I thought I might hear from, but didn't. I ran into him at a function in Toronto some time later and he was embarrassed to say that he might be famous and successful but that unfortunately he wasn't very good with his money. "I would be a hypocrite if I tried to give other people financial advice," he said. Another person I sent a letter to later told me, "If you want financial advice, ask my ex-wife. She's got all the money." To me this was a bit of a wake-up call that while it may appear you are successful, your bank account could be near empty. This is, of course, true of how many Canadians are living today.

● ● ● ● ● ●

One of my favourite quotes came from Alberta Premier Ralph Klein. In a province rich with resources he has led a government that has its fiscal house in order. It's also Canada's only province that doesn't have a provincial sales tax. Klein compares running a province to running a household.

Albertans have a long-standing reputation for being fiscally conservative, and that tendency has always been reflected in my government's approach to handling the province's finances and spending taxpayer dollars. If I could share one piece of advice with Canadians interested in becoming wise consumers and saving money, it would be this: When my government first began working to get Alberta's fiscal house in order, we quickly realized that the province did not have a revenue problem; it had a spending problem. We spent years paying off deficit and debt and Albertans had to sacrifice to get back into the black. My advice is simple: never spend what you do not have. It is far better ... to put off a purchase for three months until you can afford it than to spend the next six months paying it off. Do not line the pockets of your bank; line your own!

● ● ● ● ● ●

Canadian rocker Sass Jordan, who topped the music charts throughout the 1980s and '90s, is now a judge scouting new talent on the hugely popular *Canadian Idol.* Jordan comes across as a very caring person, so it was no surprise that she had some good advice to pass on to Canadians who want to get ahead. (I especially like the "buy pre-owned" line, Sass!)

In my opinion, the wisest investment you could ever make is in yourself. Whatever attracts you as a career, invest in that. If you are drawn to a particular career, invest in educating yourself about it, everything about it. The knowledge you accumulate will pay off huge dividends as you age. Use one credit card, and one only. Pay it off every month. Ownership is key as well, unless it is something you are prepared to pay for as a form of convenience. Buy pre-owned as much as possible while you build your wealth. You prosper once you believe that you can.

● ● ● ● ● ●

Who would know more about money than a CEO of a Canadian bank? John Hunkin was president and CEO of Canadian Imperial Bank of Commerce until he stepped down last year. He told me the key to financial success was to save and save early.

> If there is one piece of financial advice I would give people, it would be to save and invest as early as possible in life. Thanks to the magic of compound interest and the track record of equity investment growth over the mid to long term, this is the best single move that one can make.

• • • • • •

CTV's Lloyd Robertson is Canada's most trusted news anchor and in case you didn't know it, he's also a very nice guy. I asked Lloyd if there was anything he could pass on to the average Canadian regarding finances, and he told me that he learned the value of money early. Robertson was born during the Great Depression and his father instilled in him that he should hang onto any job he might get, work hard and save his money.

> I can recall that my first job was after school and Saturdays at the Dufferin Market in my hometown of Stratford, Ontario. I delivered groceries on a bicycle and stocked shelves. One early spring day, with a big box of goods stacked in a cardboard box on my bike's carrier, I went spinning out of control on a patch of black ice and smashed onto the roadway. I picked up a couple of bruises but, more importantly, the groceries spilled all over the street and a large glass bottle of Javex broke in a hundred pieces and the smelly liquid oozed its way through the celery, apples and potatoes. Twelve dollars worth of supplies, a lot of money in the late 1940s, was completely ruined. There was never any question that the money would come out of my pay. Since I was making about $4.50 a week, it took me three weeks to pay off the store. It was a lesson learned in the true value of the dollar.

• • • • • •

James (Jimmy) Pattison is a Vancouver-based entrepreneur who is the chairman, president, CEO and sole owner of the Jim Pattison Group, one of Canada's largest privately held companies. Growing up he sold magazine subscriptions and garden seeds door to door, and while attending university he washed cars and worked at a used car lot. He worked his way up to owning a car dealership, which then turned into 13 dealerships. He eventually expanded his empire into transportation, communications, food products, packaging, real estate, financial services and the Ripley's Believe It or Not! museums. His company currently has a net value of $5.2 billion and employs 26,000 people in 48 countries—not bad for someone who started out selling garden seeds door to door. I asked Pattison what advice he could give the rest of us to be successful.

> I have never met anyone who was successful at anything who didn't work extremely hard. If you are going to be a good violin player you have to practise. If you work hard and force yourself to save money early in life, then I don't think you can miss. But you have to want it to succeed. It has to come from within.

• • • • • •

Galen Weston and his family have a net worth of about $8.7 billion, second only to Kenneth Thomson and the Thomson family, who have a net worth of $22 billion. Weston runs the food empire George Weston Limited and owns Loblaw Companies Limited, the largest food retailer in Canada. He oversees more than 10,900 supermarkets operating under the Atlantic Superstore, SaveEasy, Dominion, Maxi, Provigo, Fortinos, Loblaws, Zehrs, No Frills, Valu Mart, Extra Foods, Your Independent Grocer and The Real Canadian Superstore banners. I would guess that Weston is a sailor and I thank him for this bit of advice, which he must call on when there are storms on the horizon in the boardroom.

> 'Tis the set of the sails and not the gales that determine the way they go.

• • • • • •

He may not be the financially richest man in Canada but Philip Mahr with World Vision is definitely one of the richest in spirit and one of the most impressive people I have ever met. When I traveled to Uganda with World Vision to take part in a project to renovate a centre where children of war would be rehabilitated, Philip Mahr was in charge of ensuring our group was kept safe and that we got the job done. Mahr has traveled to more than 75 countries around the world, helping eradicate poverty and bringing about a better standard of living for the world's poor. I remembered this quote from Mahr as he spoke under the hot African sun about the people he has met in his travels around the globe.

> I've traveled the world and I've seen greedy rich people and generous poor people. I've also seen generous rich people and greedy poor people.

• • • • • •

One of my favourite paintings is one called *Pancho* by Canadian artist Ken Danby. You may be more familiar with *At the Crease*, the famous painting of a goalie standing in front of a hockey net, waiting for the action to happen. That print is hanging in tens of thousands of homes across Canada. Danby is one of this county's greatest artists and I was pleased that he agreed to pass on some advice to help his fellow Canadians.

> As an artist, my focus is always on the creation of my work and the means to achieve it. Therefore, I must also remain aware of my ability to financially sustain my efforts by thinking ahead, rather than simply month by month. As a result, my commitments are planned at least a year in advance, knowing what can be successfully achieved in that period. I never use credit cards for borrowing—only for convenience and record keeping—so the monthly balance is always paid without incurring interest. My philosophy is that every day is a learning experience, as is every painting that I create. Therefore, my best work will always be my next, which is the only criteria that can attempt to ensure my future.

• • • • • •

Moses Znaimer is the internationally known Canadian broadcaster who helped change the television landscape with the launch of Citytv in Toronto. He is responsible for the creation of MuchMusic, Bravo! and MusiquePlus, as well as many other television channels and productions. He has been in the forefront of television programming, developing shows and talent. He is not just a broadcaster but also an entrepreneur, quitting the CBC to start up Toronto's first UHF station, Channel 57, in 1972, now known as Citytv. Znaimer's distinctive visionary style is now being copied across the country and around the world. When I asked Znaimer for advice for the average Canadian, he said to be the boss, do something you love and eventually you will make money at it.

> In my opinion, the most important thing is autonomy. Bosses live longer. It's a fact. So my advice is, forget the job. Start something for yourself; something that expresses you in the sense that you'd be doing it even if it didn't make you lots of money. Whatever it is, stick with it, suffer as you must, but know that the problems will eventually yield and you will get rich in spirit as well as in stuff. Remember, it's important to make money as well as things. That proves that someone other than you cares for the work. But it's equally important to make things, useful things, as well as money, because financial jiggery-pokery soon leads to business and social sterility.

● ● ● ● ● ●

Alex Trebek, the host of the popular game show *Jeopardy* is a proud Canadian who hails from Sudbury, Ontario. He's a busy man but did take the time to fax me this quote. (I'll take how to be careful with money for 100, Alex.)

> Pay off your credit cards every month and be careful when asked to invest in large projects.

● ● ● ● ● ●

Jim O'Connell with Report on Business Television is a former international correspondent with CTV and as host of ROBTV interviews top newsmakers of the day about breaking business stories. O'Connell gave this advice for Canadians who want to get ahead:

> Embrace your work and life with enthusiasm and integrity and always remember, attitude is everything.

• • • • • •

Jeff Healey is a Canadian artist who has an international reputation as a guitarist and singer. Born with a rare form of cancer called retinoblastoma, he was blind by the age of one. He received his first guitar at age three and learned to play it lap-style because his hand wasn't large enough to grip the guitar's neck. A Juno Award winner and Grammy nominee, Healey does charity work including representing The Canadian National Institute for the Blind and running its annual golf tournament every year since 1993. He now concentrates on jazz and tours the country with other accomplished jazz musicians. I spoke with him by phone when he was touring western Canada.

> It almost seems the more successful you become the more debt you have. My grandmother survived with very little money and no credit cards. But this seems to be the way our society has gone. The way we have set ourselves up is that debt seems to be part of our lives. Car leases, no money down, no payments for a year, it just seems to be part of our society and it's a very easy trap to fall into. We are all in this together. Everyone has debt. My best advice is to buckle down, work hard and get yourself a good accountant.

• • • • • •

Alexander Shnaider is a soft-spoken Toronto billionaire who, despite his enormous wealth, tries to remain low key; that is, as low key as he can be while driving $400,000 sports cars, flying in his luxury jet and buying and selling steel mills in Europe. Russian by birth and Canadian by upbringing, he is the director of the Midland Group. Shnaider is currently bankrolling development of the Trump International Hotel & Tower, a $500-million, five-star, 68-storey development in the heart of downtown Toronto. He also spent $50 million to buy a Formula One racing team. Not bad for a guy who as a child stocked shelves and mopped floors in his parents' deli. What advice does this self-made billionaire have for the rest of us?

> My keys to success can be summed up with the following simple truths: Work as hard as you can while you still can. Don't put off until tomorrow what can be done today, as tomorrow always brings new challenges. Always seek to improve. And finally, stay true to your word—it's the most valuable asset you possess.

• • • • • •

Ed Mirvish, or "Honest Ed" as he is known, is one of Toronto's most interesting characters. A charismatic person who loves the media and public attention, he has a rags-to-riches story. Mirvish came from a poor family and had to share his bathroom with up to 50 people during his childhood. What began as a small store in 1948 grew into Honest Ed's and now takes up a Toronto block. He now also owns several theatres in Toronto, including the Royal Alexandra Theatre, which was built in 1993 for $22 million. The first time I met Mirvish was at one of his turkey giveaways, which I covered for CTV early in my career. I asked Mirvish what advice he would pass on to Canadians trying to get ahead.

> I would say if you ever have the urge to make money don't fight it, it's not all that bad. In many of my public addresses over the years young people would often ask me, how can they succeed? Are there still opportunities to become successful and make money? My answer was and is "Find something you enjoy to work at, something that interests and motivates you, work at it diligently and you will succeed." With the technology we have today there are more opportunities to succeed than ever before.

• • • • • •

Allan Slaight is the executive chairman of the Standard Broadcasting Corporation. The son of a veteran newspaperman, he is a radio pioneer now in Canada's Broadcast Hall of Fame. Slaight has a long history in the broadcasting business, beginning as a reporter/announcer and working his way through the ranks of news director and general sales manager to eventually become vice president and general manager of CHUM-AM/FM. Standard Broadcasting Corporation Limited is now one of the largest privately owned multimedia companies in Canada. At the Juno Awards in April 2005, the Canadian Academy of Recording Arts and Sciences honoured him for his never-ending dedication to the Canadian radio industry. When I asked Slaight for advice to help the average Canadian, his answer was short and to the point.

> Surround yourself with the right people so there are many slaps on the back and no kicks in the arse.

● ● ● ● ● ●

I did a story on beer wars in Ontario and interviewed an impressive young entrepreneur, Manjit Minhas, president of the Lakeshore Creek Brewing Company. At 24 years old she is taking on Canada's traditional big brewers, bringing new, competitively priced beers to market to compete against Canada's major brands. The company she started in university now does $30 million a year in business. I asked her what advice she had for the average Canadian.

> As a consumer we have been branded to the nth degree. In my estimation we pay 30% to 40% more for brand-name products that are somehow supposed to make us feel cool, sexy or just plain smart. If buying a brand-name product means having the assurance of buying a product that proves to have a good cost-to-benefit ratio, lasts longer, looks better, tastes better, etc., then I am all for brand-name products. But this isn't so all the time, so I cannot understand why Canadians buy these brands of beer from companies that spend hundreds of millions of dollars in advertising to convince consumers that these beers will attract people of

the opposite sex, make you patriotic or help you join a hip crowd. Remember, just because you pay more does not mean it is a superior product; it just means the company makes more profit margin. If consumers followed this simple principle it would keep millions of dollars in their pockets.

If possible, never borrow money from a bank or any other individual because it will give you a false sense of how much money you have and are making, never mind the high interest rates you will have to pay back. If you only spend what you have in cold, hard cash, you will never be in debt or spread yourself too thin. Also, remember each penny counts because they are the ones that add up to dollars, so watch your costs very closely.

● ● ● ● ● ●

Ted Rogers is the hands-on leader of the media empire Rogers Communications Inc., which has controlling stakes in Rogers Media, Rogers Wireless and Rogers Cable. In 1960, while still a student, Rogers bought Toronto radio station CHFI—the first FM radio station in Canada—for $85,000. Rogers broadcasting operations now include 43 radio stations across Canada, two multicultural television stations in Ontario and an 80% interest in Sportsnet and The Shopping Channel, as well as interests in countless other enterprises, including the Rogers Centre in Toronto, formerly known as SkyDome. While Rogers is clearly a business icon, when I asked him to share financial advice with his fellow Canadians he wanted to speak about the importance of charity.

One of the things I am most passionate about is individuals and business supporting the community. I began early when I didn't have a lot of money but I really thought it was important. I started a scholarship fund at the University of Toronto in honour of my father, 35 years ago, with a few hundred dollars. I added to it year after year and slowly built it up so we could afford two annual scholarships. And obviously we've made significant contributions lately.

You, your family and your business exist in a community. Our community supports and encourages you—we must give back to it and it doesn't always have to be money. Give your time! Become passionate about your community.

●　●　●　●　●　●　●

While many of these successful Canadians are now household names, most started with little, and it was only their tenacity and sheer determination that propelled them to the top of their careers and professions. Their success has brought wealth not only to them, but to countless others who have been able to benefit from their vision. I wanted to speak with them because too often, people assume that the successful and rich are that way because it came easy to them. That's almost never the case and even those born with a silver spoon in their mouth must manage their wealth carefully or what they have can be lost in a generation. I have always felt it was wrong to blame poor people for being poor, and I believe it's also wrong to blame rich people for being rich. Not all us of can attain the greatness that some of these Canadians have been able to achieve, but it does show that hard work and perseverance pays off. Their advice is inspiration to us all and I thank them for their words of wisdom.

CHAPTER 3

checking in with the wealthy barber

David Chilton couldn't have imagined the impact his book *The Wealthy Barber* would have on the finances of a generation of Canadians. Having sold more than two million copies in North America, it's the best-selling book in Canadian publishing. In it, Chilton tells the fictional story of a small-town barber named Roy who uses a common sense approach to save money and build wealth.

The book is not filled with new techniques, complex strategies or get-rich-quick schemes; instead, it focuses on the basics of financial planning that when put into practice can make anyone wealthy over time. Years ago my brother, Bill, gave me Chilton's book and after reading it I embarked on a forced savings plan that enabled me to save tens of thousands of dollars. I wanted to check in with Chilton to see if anything has changed since he first wrote *The Wealthy Barber* in 1989.

"I'm the first to admit *The Wealthy Barber* is not an original thought," Chilton says. "In fact it was basically the conventional wisdom of financial planning repackaged to make it more acceptable." He adds, "As far as my philosophies on saving, they really haven't changed a whole lot. It's difficult to argue against preauthorized chequing and payroll deduction, as both have made a lot of people a lot of money over the years." That was Roy the barber's advice. "Wealth beyond your wildest dreams is possible if you follow the golden rule: Invest ten per cent of all you make for long-term growth. If you follow that one simple guideline, someday you'll be a very rich man." He may have been a fictional barber but people took that approach to heart.

Chilton claims, "The one thing that I did aggressively switch from most other books and most other planners was the approach to budgeting, and that's only because when dealing with hundred of clients when I was a broker/planner briefly in my early 20s, I realized that very few people can budget successfully. It's great in theory but seldom works in practice and that's when I recognized that forced savings has to play a major roll."

Chilton believed then and still does now that we should all be paying ourselves first. Most of us who are drowning in debt or paddling to keep our head above water pay our bills on time. We don't miss payments to the phone, cable and electric company, nor do we skip mortgage or rent payments. Paying yourself first means that making a payment to you is as critical as one to the gas company. Chilton says, "I guess I didn't recognize it at the time but it ended up that the major contribution of *The Wealthy Barber* was that it moved people away from budgeting and towards forced savings. The argument in *The Wealthy Barber* was save your 10%, put some money in your RRSP and shorten your mortgage's amortization. These are all forced savings techniques ... how you spend the rest of your money is frankly none of my business."

Of course if people just spent the money that was left over from their paycheques after paying all the bills there wouldn't be a problem. The dilemma facing a growing number of Canadians is that "keeping up with the Joneses" has driven them so far into debt that despite using an aggressive saving strategy they're not much further ahead. Chilton agrees, saying,

The one problem with forced savings and for that matter any approach to saving is that it can still be overwhelmed by debt and by lack of discipline on the spending side. If a person goes beyond spending the rest of his money and spends way more than the rest by piling on a tremendous amount of debt, especially high-interest debt, this can lead to serious financial problems. We've certainly seen a lot of people fall victim to that. There is no doubt the easy availability of money through incredible credit card availability, through debit cards, through easy withdrawals and through cheap money with low interest rates has hurt people. Keeping up with the Joneses, which was a problem in 1989 when I wrote the book, has now become an epidemic. In fact, staying ahead of the Jones is the objective of most people.

A problem area that I am seeing more often as a consumer advocate and that I will discuss more fully later in this book is the home equity loan or credit line. Bank lenders practically fall over themselves trying to get you to sign documents that will give you access to thousands of dollars of credit from the equity in your home. Chilton is of the same opinion. "Funnily enough, one issue that I see jumping up a lot is credit lines. Credit lines for the undisciplined are like a large credit card. Yes, they're a lower interest rate but they're still very damaging for people. For some reason when people get a credit line they treat it like it's already their money. They forget that it's borrowed money."

Chilton is optimistic that consumers can get a handle on their finances and says most of the people he deals with come to the realization they can't spend more than they make—another one of Roy the barber's common sense guidelines. "The vast majority of people that I deal with have handled their finances quite well and have applied the principles of *The Wealthy Barber* and other very good books and have worked with financial planners to successfully put forced savings to good use. The sad tale is there is no way for a book to stop [their] overspending. That requires a lot of self-discipline and almost personal coaching."

Chilton becomes philosophical when I ask him what he feels consumers are going to have to do to get a handle on their finances if they are overwhelmed by debt. "We all have to buckle down and try to find some joy in non-materialistic goods. I don't mean to sound like a New Age thinker because I'm not at all, but that really is the problem that most people have. As corny as it sounds, what people have to do is stop caring so much about stuff. It's funny; the older I get, the more I realize that good financial planning is less about the intricate knowledge of the stock market and forecasting future interest rates and more and more about discipline and not wanting so much stuff."

Well said, David. I don't think Roy the barber could have put it better himself.

CHAPTER 4

living next door to a millionaire

When two researchers set out to interview the wealthy in America they combed through affluent neighbourhoods on streets dotted with extravagant homes, luxury vehicles parked out front and in-ground swimming pools in the backyard. They were shocked to find out that the people living in these homes were not wealthy.

Thomas Stanley and William Danko discovered in their research for *The Millionaire Next Door*, a bestseller that has sold more than three million copies, that many of the millionaires in the United States are not necessarily living in what most of us would consider upscale housing. Instead, millionaires are in modest homes, working and living next door to people who have a fraction of their wealth.

The millionaires next door are not handed their riches, either. Stanley and Danko discovered that 80% of America's wealthy are first-generation rich. They are compulsive savers and investors.

Stanley and Danko found seven factors that they believe help someone becomea millionaire. These factors are as relevant here as they are south of the border.

1. They live well below their means.
2. They allocate their time, energy and money efficiently, in ways conducive to building wealth.
3. They believe that financial independence is more important that displaying high social status.
4. Their parents did not provide economic outpatient care (their moms and dads didn't pay the kids' bills).
5. Their adult children are economically self-sufficient.
6. They are proficient in targeting market opportunities.
7. They chose the right occupation.

● ● ● ● ● ●

I got the chance to talk to author William Danko about the success of the book and how he feels about his research 10 years after it was first published. Danko says, "When I look at my own life I've done very well with my research. I was doing fine before *The Millionaire Next Door* as well. I was consulting and I'm still a professor of marketing at the University at Albany, State University of New York. I still have the same spouse of 30 years. I still have the same house. I have three well-educated, emancipated kids that don't ask me for money. Things are good. I practise what I preach. I still don't have cable television—I couldn't afford it 30 years ago and I don't need it now."

It's estimated that in the United States, about one of 15 households—that's 8.2 million households out of 110 million— would be considered a millionaire household. Conversely, 14 out of 15 are not even close to a million. "When you look at the anatomy of that one out of 15, you find that these millionaires are living in ordinary housing and not calling attention to themselves. They believe that financial security is more important than outward man-ifestations," says Danko.

The original research on millionaires still resonates 10 years later and is likely to stand the test of time. What Stanley and Danko found was that the neighbourhoods they assumed were filled with wealthy people were not. Many of the huge homes had huge mort-gages. The luxury cars were leased and while the occupants had high salaries they had no net worth. Notes Danko, "We called this big hat—no cattle." While they were surprised, there was no argu-ing with the data and that's when they had to face the fact that many millionaires were living in regular, traditional neighbourhoods. "We had a number of surveys, government information and per-sonal interviews that consistently gave the same result, so we had convergent validity—that's when you have multiple data sources converging on the same basic truth. It just bolsters the argument even more."

So what does the man who studied millionaires have to say about the road to riches? "Live on 80% of what you make. If you can systematically save and invest 20% of whatever you are making and let the time value of money work for you, you can't lose. That's what we mean by frugality." Many people who are strapped with debt are looking for a magic bullet, something that will make them say, "Ahhh, yes, here is how I can get out of debt and continue the free-spending ways I have become accustomed to." It won't happen without lifestyle changes. "It really is [about] buckling down and living on less," claims Danko, "yet no one wants to hear the hard medicine and begin doing that. How in the world can you be an investor and let the time value of money work for you with com-pounding if you are not a saver? And how can you be a saver if you are in debt?"

Americans are struggling with their consumer debt the same as we Canadians are. The median household income in the U.S. is about $43,000 a year and Americans are spending about $45,000 a year. In Canada, the median income is about $60,000 and we are spending at the same rate. Only about 1% of total income is being saved, so people are digging themselves in deeper and deeper every year.

Danko says people should not worry about doom and gloom on the news and things they can't control, but instead plan for their own future. "Wars happen, terrorist attacks happen, SARS happens and the point is we all get over it. Life goes on. What you have to do is have that long-term view that you are probably going to live until 70 or 80 years of age or older and if you don't start working, saving and investing when you're young, you won't have the money you need when you are older to look after yourself and your family."

He mentions that Franco Modigliani won a Nobel Prize for his work studying the life cycle of money. In its simplest form, Danko explains, Modigliani was saying that when you are young, you work for money, and when you are old, money works for you. This is exactly how Benjamin Franklin laid out his life. The American who became famous for being a scientist, inventor, statesman, printer, philosopher, musician and economist once said he was going to retire from Congress at the age of 42 and live on his interest and dividends, and he did. Danko said, "He turned his life to productive things like inventions and other public works. He [understood]." (I'll have more on Franklin in the following pages as many of the things he said 250 years ago ring true today.)

Danko suggests that while old-fashioned virtues can guide us today regarding money management, he would add three additional points to wealth building.

Those include a good marriage, good health and good income. A good marriage, if it really is good, gives you greater life satisfaction and greater life satisfaction adds to a longer life and a longer life allows for greater compounding opportunities. If you are making a good income and you are consistently saving that 20%, over time it's really hard not to make a fortune. If you have a bad marriage and you find yourself in divorce court, at a minimum you will lose half of your assets. I interviewed one physician who made a good living but he made most of his money in real estate. He used to be worth $60 million; now he's worth $30 million.

He adds that if you're young and savvy enough to be a good saver, despite government activities, worldwide disease, natural disasters and terrorism, and consistently make a commitment to live below your means, then again, you can't lose.

The man that has interviewed thousands of high-net-worth individuals (HNWIs, loosely defined as people with one million investable dollars) also has some other interesting perspectives on wealth, including the fact that money doesn't always change you, but it does change the people around you. Danko says he interviewed a man who was worth $20 million because of an invention he made. He married for love and had two daughters prior to striking it rich. Danko says, "He had to move from his community, because everybody thought he was just a lucky son of a gun. So he moved to a new place, started a new life with his family and now tries to keep a low profile. He can do anything he wants, but he just wants to try and live a normal life."

Danko's latest research is about quality of life, which he has entitled *Richer Than a Millionaire*. He studied 1,400 HNWIs and reviewed value issues concerning their spouses, children, parents, and even religions, spirituality and life satisfaction. He says, "I'm looking at those people who are rich but miserable, as well as rich and happy. Of course, being rich and happy is where you want to be." Danko studied a group of very happy up-and-coming millionaires with a net worth between $100,000 and a million dollars who can't quite retire, but they're not hard scrabble either. There was also a group between $100,000 and a million dollars who are miserable. Danko says, "Well, when I look at those up and comers who are very happy I will take their life day any of the week as opposed to someone who becomes a millionaire yet belongs to that rich and miserable group."

Danko believes that if people can get a handle on their spending and make an effort to save 10% to 20% of their income, they, too, can become the millionaires next door. He says, "The basic truths never go out of style. Hard work and perseverance. While no one wants to hear that, it is the reality. Some people may say he just got lucky. Well, sure, maybe luck is part of it. But I would say the harder I work, the luckier I get."

For more information on Danko's projects, check out his website at http://www.albany.edu/~danko.

Throughout this book I will be providing practical advice as well as excellent information from Canadian experts who can tell us how to put Danko's research to good use. Investing wisely, being frugal and setting aside a portion of your income for the future are global strategies that are applicable not just in the U.S., but in any other country in the world, including Canada. In the pages ahead we will discuss how you too can become "the millionaire next door."

CHAPTER 5

finding out what makes Canadian millionaires tick

As we just learned from *The Millionaire Next Door* by Thomas Stanley and William Danko, not all millionaires drive around in flashy cars, sport Rolex watches and spend their weekends lounging aboard luxury yachts. In fact, most drive Ford pick-ups, live in modest homes and shop at Sears. Stanley and Danko also found that 80% of millionaires are first-generation rich. They made it on their own. Accumulating wealth takes discipline, sacrifice and hard work, and most importantly, *millionaires live well below their means*! The situation is no different here in Canada.

Thane Stenner is known as Canada's "advisor to the wealthy," and is therefore uniquely qualified to tell us about Canadian millionaires. He is the leader of the T. Stenner Group, a team of specialists that provide wealth management solutions to millionaires and their families, and he is also a first vice-president of CIBC Wood Gundy in Vancouver. He's also co-author with James Dolan of *True Wealth: An Expert Guide for High-Net-Worth Individuals (And Their Advisors)*, a book to help millionaires deal with the complexities and strategies of their enormous wealth. It's a book that tells you not how to get rich, but what to do once you are. (It would help to be wealthy, as the book sells for $80 a copy.)

Stenner classifies someone as wealthy (an HNWI) if they have at least $1 million in investable assets. This does not include the house, cottage and RRSPs; it's $1 million free and clear that can be used to generate new wealth. Currently, there are approximately 350,000 Canadians that would be considered in this range and the number is growing every year. Those individuals with $10 million or more in investable assets are ultra-high-net-worth individuals or UHNWIs. Canadians with a bankroll that includes more than $100 million in investable assets are called superwealthy (I think we can all agree with that).

> While the number of millionaires fluctuates from year to year it's estimated that 40% of Canada's millionaires live in Ontario, 23% in Quebec, 16% in British Columbia and 12% in Alberta.

So what can Canadian millionaires teach the rest of us? "There are many things that the average Canadian can learn from the habits of Canadian millionaires," says Stenner. "First and foremost they are not prone to overconsumption. In almost all cases they are ready to sacrifice something today in order to achieve greater wealth and prosperity in the future."

Stenner says when it comes to wealth it's what is in the investment account that counts, not what is on the paycheque. "There are a lot of people who look wealthy. They drive fancy cars, live in upscale homes and wear expensive suits but when you examine their true wealth it's a different story."

In dealing with Canadian millionaires, Stenner learned what the authors of the *The Millionaire Next Door* found earlier: Many Canadian millionaires have small, community-based businesses, reside in reasonably priced neighbourhoods and live well below their means. People who have a six-figure salary but nothing to show for it are not wealthy; they are just living high. Many successful Canadians millionaires are business owners and entrepreneurs who have used leverage wisely to get ahead. But Stenner says you don't have to own a company to get into the millionaire's circle and that if someone is prudent with their wealth, it's possible to use an average income to accumulate an above-average net worth.

The T. Stenner Group *Millionaires Survey* offers a fascinating perspective into how Canada's wealthy think. It's an inside look at the attitudes of Canada's high-net-worth individuals. In one question, the survey asks the rich what they actually think about the process of attaining and securing their wealth. The two top results show that in most cases Canadian millionaires want what we all want: the sense of long-term security and peace of mind that wealth provides. They also are pleased that their wealth allows them to have a comfortable lifestyle that provides advantages for family members.

The actual survey is conducted by interviewing hundreds of millionaires and is an ongoing document that also details how millionaires feel about the service they receive from their financial advisors. While the survey is extensive, I have included some questions and answers from 2004 that I feel can benefit those of us aspiring to be millionaires.

The first question asked the rich what they like about being rich.

Please rank the following benefits of wealth in order of importance to you. Results:

1   Allows me to live comfortably and where I choose
2   Gives me long-term security and peace of mind
3   Allows me to provide advantages for my family
4   Allows me to enjoy luxuries such as travel and recreation
5   Enables me to maintain good health and access to medical expertise
6   Allows me to leave an inheritance to my family members or others
7   Allows me to support charitable causes

This question asks the rich how they got rich.

What is your primary source of wealth? What is your secondary source of wealth?
Results:

		Primary source %	Secondary source %
1	Earnings from a business	30.3%	19.9%
2	Earnings from a professional practice	10.3%	12.4%
3	Real estate holdings	9.8%	8.5%
4	Sale of business	8.1%	3.0%
5	Inheritance	9.4%	9.0%
6	Stock or stock options in employer corporations	5.1%	7.5%
7	Sale of real estate	6.8%	10.0%
8	Other	10.7%	10.4%

This question asks Canadian millionaires about their annual household income. It's particularly telling that while all of the people surveyed are millionaires, more than 60% spend less than $250,000 annually. This is a huge figure for most of us, but is also an indicator that many Canadian millionaires are living well below their means and could spend much more if they wanted to.

What is your household's average income from all sources?
Results:

Average household annual income

Less than $100,000	12.4%
Between $100,000 and $250,000	49.3%
Between $250,000 and $400,000	16.9%
Between $400,000 and $500,000	8.0%
Between $500,000 and $1,000,000	5.8%
Between $1,000,000 and $2,000,000	4.0%
Greater than $2,000,000	3.6%

And what do these Canadian millionaires do with their time? Many of them are business owners and retirees.

What is your current occupation?

Results:

Primary occupation

Business owner	30.6%
Retiree	23.3%
Corporate executive	14.7%
Partner in a professional firm	7.8%
Sports/entertainment/media	1.7%
Medical/dental practitioner	0.9%
Other	21.1%

The following question also shows that wealthy people are no different from the rest of us when it comes to worrying about money. While one-fifth of Canadian millionaires never have to worry about the handling of expenses, such as paying bills, fixing the roof, buying groceries and paying other household bills, 65.4% worry sometimes and 13.2% worry a lot about their wealth.

Please indicate whether or not you spend time worrying about handling your household wealth.

Results:

Amount of worry about handling household wealth

A lot	13.2%
Sometimes	65.4%
Basically never	21.4%

The Stenner survey also asked Canadian millionaires to rank what worries them.

What is it that you currently worry about?

Results:

1   Lower future returns on my investments

2   Unpredictability of the return my investments will provide over the long term

3   I won't be able to maintain the income level to which I have become accustomed

4   My following generations will have a more difficult time financially than I did

5   Terrorism and how it will affect the economy, the markets and therefore my investments

6   Terrorism and how it will affect my personal security and that of my family

7   Education costs for my children and grandchildren

8   Uncertainty about estate taxes

...and how many financial advisors they use. This just goes to show that even millionaires admit they don't know everything about money.

How many advisors/counsellors does your household use regularly to manage its wealth?

Results:

Number of advisors/counsellors used

None, it is done by myself	17.6%
One advisor	38.2%
Two advisors	32.6%
Three advisors	6.9%
More than three advisors	4.7%

There is no quicker way to divide wealth in a household than a divorce. Not surprisingly then, many Canadian millionaires are married.

What is your marital status?

Results:

Marital status

Marital status	
Married	76.2%
Single	8.9%
Divorced	6.8%
Widowed	4.3%
Common law	3.8%

The survey finds that Canadian millionaires are frugal but are proud of their accomplishments, and they do tend to enjoy their wealth when they feel they have attained a certain level of success and security. Stenner says, "Canadian millionaires like to spend money at some point in their lives. But they are willing to make sacrifices early in life so that they can enjoy their wealth later. This also allows them to have security for their families as well." Stenner continues, "The key is delayed consumption. Keep in mind that people are living longer, so someone who is 40 years old could live another 50 years. People can use this time to save and accumulate wealth. They will want, as well, to ensure they have enough money in their retirement." Stenner says one aspect benefiting Canadian families is that nowadays, people are more willing to discuss finances openly and teach their children ways to save money and build wealth, whereas the people who went through the Great Depression didn't speak freely about issues like money.

Another interesting thing Stenner has noticed after working with Canadian millionaires is that money amplifies the kind of person you are. "If someone is a generous person before they become wealthy, they will be even more generous after they attain wealth." He says it's conversely true that a miser will become more miserly. In his book *True Wealth* he breaks down Canadian millionaires into groups that reflect their personality.

The Caregiver (20% of the millionaire population): Someone with a strong desire to provide for the family and who is generous and charitable with money.

The Runaway (17%): Someone who is stressed, anxious and worried about their wealth and would rather have professionals manage it.

The Libertarian (13%): A highly motivated, focused individual whose sole goal is financial freedom.

The Recluse (12%): An intensely private person who wants to keep it that way.

The Boss (10%): A strong, aggressive person who wants to control all financial decisions.

The Superstar (8%): A status-oriented individual who uses money as a source of their identity and has big spending habits.

The Empire Builder (8%): A focused, performance-driven investor who uses money as a measure of success.

The Player (6%): A high-risk individual who sees investing as a game that offers excitement as well as opportunity.

The Academic (6%): Someone with a strong desire to be innovative and invest in new products. He or she feels that being wealthy means being knowledgeable and well informed.

What Stenner's research tells us is that millionaires are really no different than the rest of us. They want to provide for their families. They want security for the future. They want to live comfortably and have good health. When they feel the time has come to reward themselves they do it with luxuries or vacations. What may be different about Canadian millionaires and the rest of us is their work ethic, discipline and their ability to live well below their means.

What else can we take from this research? Well, if 80% of millionaires are first-generation rich, we all have the ability to become millionaires. Even if you can't bank a million you can still save enough to achieve what these millionaires have: safety, security and peace of mind. In the pages that follow we will look at the strategies necessary to become part of this select group. More detailed information on the *Millionaires Survey*, the T. Stenner Group and Thane Stenner's book, *True Wealth*, can be found at www.truewealth.ca.

asking an expert what the economic future holds

We need to get a hold of our finances and take command over our debt because no one knows what the economy will be throwing our way. As interest rates hit a 40-year low a few years ago, consumers began racking up record debts with record spending. A spike in interest rates now could be disastrous for the many Canadians who are saddled with debt. Anyone having trouble paying off loans and lines of credit when rates are low could find themselves forced out of their homes and into bankruptcy if rates increase steadily over a short period.

While there is no crystal ball regarding the future of interest rates, there are certainly some economists with the inside track after decades of intense scrutiny of world economies, stock markets and real estate cycles. One of Canada's foremost economists is Jeffery Rubin. He is the chief economist and strategist for CIBC World Markets and was a senior policy advisor for Ontario's finance ministry from 1982 to 1988. Rubin has always been a respected voice, but he sealed his reputation as someone who should be listened to when he predicted "the real estate bubble would burst" in 1989, just before it did. At the time, many thought the red-hot real estate market would never slow down, but it did and in a hurry. Now when Rubin talks people listen. I spoke with him about the huge amount of consumer debt being carried by Canadians, his thoughts on interest rates and the current real estate market, and whether or not the real estate market bubble could burst as well.

As housing prices continue to rise unabated, consumers continue to take equity out of their homes to spend it, plunging them into more debt and putting them at the mercy of interest rates. Rubin agrees if interest rates did rise sharply, debt-laden Canadians would be in trouble. "The lethal implications of this debt, or the potentially lethal implications of this debt, would be if we reached a level of interest rates equal to what average interest rates have been over the past 30 years. If that happened, this would be extremely challenging and troubling for our economy. However, I don't believe that's where interest rates are going. I believe, in fact, that interest rates are going even lower," states Rubin. Lower interest rates? How could that be?

Rubin says that the fact that Canadians are so debt-laden means that interest rates could never be allowed to rise sharply or it could send the entire economy into a tailspin. "There is so much consumer debt that a rise in interest rates could have catastrophic consequences on the financial positions of households, with draconian consequences for spending. This very heightened vulnerability of the economy to higher interest rates due to this huge increase in consumer debt is an anchor and will likely be an anchor on interest rates for years to come." There is almost some irony in the fact that Canadians have so much debt that interest rates can't be allowed to go up or the whole country would be in trouble.

So what about the real estate market? Does Rubin think the bubble will burst again? Monitoring what's happening south of the border is a leading indicator of what will happen here.

> Housing prices, particularly in the United States, have gone through the roof. What has happened has been a huge explosion in real estate values. They are without precedent in the last 100 years in the U.S. A big deflation in housing prices would only come with a sharp rise in interest

> rates. I think what we are going to see is that the federal reserve board, for all their rhetoric, are probably in the 8th or 9th innings of their tightening cycle, maybe one or two more to go. We may be looking at something very akin to the peak of the cycle of interest rates, in which case I don't think we are going to see the bubble burst like it did in 1989, 1990, particularly in Canada.

The likelihood that the bubble won't burst is probably great news if you are someone who has purchased a home recently or has their home heavily leveraged.

And what does one of Canada's leading economists think is likely to happen in the housing market in the near term? "Instead of a sharp drop like we saw in the stock market in 2000 or what we saw in the Canadian real estate market in 1990, I think we will see a prolonged period of stagnation in terms of stagnant real estate prices," declares Rubin. "Whether we're at that point yet remains to be seen. I personally think that point is still ahead of us."

Rubin doesn't think it's rates that will eventually lead to a decrease in housing prices. "I think the threat to real estate prices down the road will not be higher interest rates. It will be a weaker economy, a weaker economy that will be motivated by rising energy prices. How that weaker economy feeds back into real estate prices remains to be seen, but most likely it will have some feedback."

Rubin wants to make it clear that all the overspending by Canadians is not a positive thing. He does, however, believe the massive debt load taken on by consumers at this point is manageable. "I'm not saying this is a good thing to have all this consumer debt. What I am saying is that with low interest or even lower rates it need not be a lethal thing for the economy. If interest rates remain low and indeed go lower, it's probably a debt that most consumers will be able to carry," says Rubin.

If you are someone loaded with debt, this may sound like good news. Lower interest rates for years to come, no bubble bursting in the housing market and the fact that the government must handle the economy with kid gloves because everyone has so much debt could give us all extra time to pay off our debt. It means you have a fighting chance to get your debt under control.

Take advantage of this opportunity, because rates won't stay low forever. Rubin adds, "At some point interest rates will go up and when they do, people are going to have to de-leverage in a big hurry."

I also asked Rubin, as one of the top officials at a large financial institution, for the single best piece of advice he would share with Canadians. He says borrow short, invest long. In other words, when you borrow money for something, go short term. Research has shown over time it's always better to take a one- or two-year mortgage than it is to lock in for five to seven years. When it's time to invest, invest for the long term. The stock market will always have its ups and downs, but over time it's been shown to outperform almost all other investments, including real estate. Rubin says,

> It's something that I have always believed in when I was a mortgage holder and something that I have always adhered to as a long bond investor, and they are really both flips sides of the same coin. When I had a mortgage, I never had a mortgage longer than a year because I believe that it never paid to get a two-, three- or five-year mortgage, so I always borrowed short. And the same difference between short- and long-term interest rates is why I've been an investor in long-term bonds. I would say the moral of the story is if you are borrowing, borrow short. And if you are investing, invest long.

Great advice. I'll address short- and long-term mortgages in a future chapter and you will see how going short over the term of mortgage can help you save tens of thousands of dollars on your home.

If you have a lot of debt, Rubin's words may be somewhat comforting, but what this really means is that we all have an opportunity to take advantage of low interest rates to pay down our debt. Every extra payment on a mortgage, line of credit or car loan will go toward paying down the principal instead of servicing debt.

Now it's time to take a good look at your overall financial picture.

calculating your financial worth

If you want to get in great physical shape you have to work at it. You have to exercise, watch what you eat and live a healthy lifestyle. If you do, you'll lose weight, gain muscles and keep your body in prime condition. If instead you lie around watching television for five hours every day, eat junk food and drive half a block to get your mail, you will be in terrible physical shape. The same is true of your financial health. If you are unsure of your net worth you will never get ahead. If you want to be a lean, mean, debt-reducing machine you will have to pay as close attention to your finances as athletes training for the Olympics pay to physical activity.

It's hard to reduce your debt and improve your net worth if you are in denial about your current financial situation. It's amazing how many people aren't sure what the interest rates are on their credit cards, what the management expense ratios are on their mutual funds or what the true cost to operate their car is. Many of us are coasting through life without taking the time to analyze our finances and look for potential savings—savings we are sure to find if we would only look! We spend 20 minutes picking out a movie at the video store, but not that amount of time going over our financial position each week. The only way to make sure we are on course to becoming debt free is to keep a close and constant eye on the money flowing in and out of our lives.

Before you can get started climbing out of debt you have to know just how big a hole you are in. This is a crucial part of your net worth plan. The big picture—your financial worth, such as mortgage, lines of credit and investments—should be examined every six months or so, while the small picture—your bills and general expenses and your strategy for reducing them—should be examined every payday.

Determining your net worth is easy. If you had to sell everything you owned and pay off every debt you had, what would you be left with? Simply subtract your assets (what you own) from your liabilities (what you owe) to determine what you're worth.

Here's an example of what this review might look like:

Assets

Savings account	$500
Chequing account	$500
Investments	
mutual funds	$5,000
stocks	$6,000
bonds	0
GICs	0
term deposits	0
Value of home	$220,000
Value of automobiles	$35,000
Property or big ticket items	
boat	$4,000
RRSPs	$20,000
Pension holdings	$15,000
Other holdings	0
Total Assets	$306,000

Liabilities

Mortgage (balance owing)	$165,000
Car loans	$23,000
Other loans	
consolidation loan	$12,000
Line of credit	$15,000
Credit cards	$5,200
Property taxes owing	0
Income taxes owing	0
Bills owing	$4,800
Other debts	$2,600
Total Liabilities	$227,600

Assets - Liabilities = Net Financial Worth
$306,000 - $227,600 = $78,400

A net worth of $78,000 might not seem too bad if you are 28 years old and starting out. It's not so great if you are 46 years old and will soon have children heading off to college or university. Nevertheless, you will not get ahead by being in the dark, so figure out what you are worth and keep a close watch on your assets and liabilities. There is comfort in watching your net worth grow and your debts disappear. Some people who do not carry out this exercise pay their credit card bills, car payments and other debts every month, while at the same time running up almost equal amounts of debt. They are stuck in a holding pattern that is not reducing debt or gaining equity. They are swimming upstream.

While you have all your investments, tax returns, bank accounts, credit card debts, loans, safety deposit box information and other important documents at hand, organize them somewhere easily accessible in case you die or become seriously ill. When you die, it would be a shame to have $10,000 sitting in an account that no one knows about. Your will, life insurance policy and financial advisor's contact information should be kept in a safe place where your family can find them. That's money that can end up in Ottawa at the Bank of Canada in the unclaimed balances division. As you will read later in the book, more than $200 million has gone astray from people not watching their money closely enough.

monitoring your expenses

Once you have established your financial worth, the most important thing you can do is monitor the amount of money that is flowing in and out of your life every month! The only way you can tell if you are getting ahead is if you write your income and expenses down and see them in black and white. It is something I do myself with every paycheque and it really does give you a true picture of the financial progress you and your family are making. Here is an example of what a monthly budget worksheet looks like for Robert and Sarah's family.

May 2006

CASH INFLOW

Robert's salary	$2,800
Sarah's salary	$1,800
Other income	0
TOTAL CASH INFLOW	$4,600

CASH OUTFLOW

Living Expenses

Mortgage	$1,400
Property taxes	$250
Phone & cell phone	$110

Natural gas	$150
Electricity	$180
Water	$85
Car insurance	$120
Home insurance	$40
Groceries	$360
Total Living Expenses	$2,695

Debt Payments

Credit card	$150
Department card	$80
Car loan	$340
Credit line interest	$58
Gas card	$50
Total Debt Payments	$678

Investments

Education funds (RESPs)	$60
RRSPs	$100
Company stock plan	$140
Total Investments	$300

Miscellaneous Expenses

Piano lessons	$60
Hockey	$50
Vacation budget	$100
Dining out	$100
Movies	$50
Golf	$120
Total Miscellaneous Expenses	$480
TOTAL CASH OUTFLOW	$4,153

Once you have these totaled you simply take your cash inflow—the amount of money coming in—and subtract the cash outflow—the amount of money going out—to determine your surplus or deficit. In Robert and Sarah's case it would look like this.

Cash Inflow - Cash Outflow = Surplus or Deficit

$4,600 - $4,153 = $447 Surplus

This budget worksheet shows that Robert and Sarah are living very close to the edge of their finances. They are saving some money in RESPs and RRSPs, but it would only take an expensive car repair, costly school trip for their kids or urgent home repair to quickly put them in a deficit situation.

Even if you don't have a major expense there are always minor ones happening throughout the month that can quickly add up to hundreds of dollars. New coats, birthday parties and medicine are just some of the unforeseen things you may not be able to budget for.

This exercise only monitors cash flow and the servicing of debt. It does not deal with the debt accumulated on charge cards, loans and lines of credit. Nevertheless, this is an important exercise that should be performed *every month* to determine your financial position and help you identify problem areas of spending.

I find what works best is to make the budget worksheet up once (leaving spaces for the amounts) and print off or photocopy 10 or 20 copies at a time that you can use over the course of the year. (Don't forget to save the budget worksheet on your computer so it's there when you need to make more copies.)

Keep a briefcase or filing cabinet dedicated to this and make the effort to complete this exercise every month. You will be glad you did. It will also help both you and your spouse keep an eye on your joint finances. This is extremely important, as you will see in our next chapter, Seeing Marriage as a Partnership.

seeing marriage as a partnership

Deciding to get married is one of the biggest decisions of your life, guided, of course, by cupid's arrow and matters of the heart. It's also the biggest business decision you will ever make. You have chosen a financial partner and will now have your own company together, a partnership. While there are many different phases and spending patterns we all go through in life, one thing is clear—marriage is just as important a partnership in the business sense as it is in the romantic one, and a couple will never get ahead financially if both people involved are not on the same page.

What good is it for a wife to scrimp and save and clip coupons if her husband is customizing an overpriced truck? Why should a husband spend long hours working overtime if his wife racks up credit card debt to wear the latest expensive fashions? All the money-saving techniques and strategies are thrown out the window if both parties are not working together, heading in the same direction.

Before embarking on any financial strategy, you and your partner should sit down and review your current financial situation. And, as discussed in the previous chapter, you should also do this on a regular basis; you both should know how much money is coming in and out of the home every month. At least once a year, perform a year-end analysis the same way a small business would. Sit down together and plan to spend an hour or more on your finances. How is it going? Are you on track? Did you have unexpected losses or, hopefully, gains?

I have always been amazed when one spouse says the other looks after all the finances and they're not really sure what is going on. Would the part owner of a company allow the other partner full access to the books without looking themself? If you are the one on the outside, you should find out exactly what is going on. If you're the bookkeeper, throw open the balance sheets to your spouse so they know your company's bottom line, whether it's good, bad or otherwise. Too many couples are running on a financial treadmill, paying off $300 in debt one month, but in the same month over-spending and adding another $300 to their credit cards. It may feel like you are getting ahead if you are paying off debt, but if you or your spouse is just racking up more debt at the same time, you'll never get ahead. That's why it is so important to sit down and look at the cold, hard figures.

One of the main things couples fight about is money, so if you want to have peace at home and keep your marriage on a solid footing, treat your marriage like a company and your spouse like a partner and your firm will prosper. It's not always easy and it's not always pleasant, but it won't do you any good to be in denial about your finances. If you do have a hard time talking about money you will have to find some way to open the lines of communication. Don't bring up money issues in the heat of an argument. Set aside time in a non-confrontational way, such as by saying, "This week-end let's talk about our financial situation. Let's do it this Sunday afternoon at two o'clock over a pot of coffee." In extreme cases you or your spouse may need counselling, but if that is what's necessary, do it.

setting goals

Depending on your current financial position, you may feel on track, concerned about your situation or totally depressed and wondering if you will ever get your head above water. No matter where you are at, it's important to set goals and then achieve them. If you think you will never get out of debt, you never will. If you envision yourself with bills paid off and money in the bank, that's what will happen. However, you have to be realistic about your goals. If you focus on a million bucks, a waterfront cottage and a new Mercedes, you will have great trouble getting there. Even a thousand-mile journey begins with a single step, and the same is true of getting your finances in order.

If you are serious about tackling debt and saving money, you need to keep track of your spending and see just how much money is flowing in and out of your life. How much do you spend in a day? In a week? You need to sit down with every paycheque and see where the money is going. You will need to reassess where you are spending your money. Is the weekly dinner out really necessary? Would monthly do? Do your children really need $120 running shoes? Wouldn't shoes at half that price be just fine? Too often people feel that their situation is so hopeless that they don't know where to start. You need to start addressing how much money you are spending right *now*! You can't change the past but you can the future.

When I was in my 20s, I decided to allocate $200 a paycheque to buy mutual funds. The first few times, my weekly spending habits sorely missed this money. It seriously affected my entertainment budget and there was less going out and fewer CDs and gadgets to buy. But after a while I didn't miss the money, and $400 a month sure adds up fast. I was able to use this money to help buy my first home. Many of us spend whatever is left over after the necessities are paid. People who make $50,000 a year tend to spend $50,000. Those who earn $120,000 a year tend to spend $120,000 or more. This is why it is so important to allocate money to pay off debt, save for your child's education and pay down your mortgage.

Throughout this book I will talk about the importance of setting goals. Your first goal may be to pay off a credit card or a car loan or to start a vacation fund. Whatever it is you will have to *stick with it*! This will be difficult when the holidays arrive and you feel you should purchase expensive gifts. You will feel the pressure when the snow arrives and you would love a week in the sun in Mexico. There will always be expenditures around the corner waiting to jump out at you and you will have to decide if they are wants or needs. Recently our daughter had a birthday party at the local grocery store. It's a new idea where the kids get to make a small cake and wear a chef's hat. It was cute and the kids had fun, but I was shocked when the bill was $380 for a two-hour party! I told my wife that next year I'll make the cake. We all deserve a good party, a vacation or a chance to reward ourselves once in a while, but you should always be looking at the big picture. Does spending this money now fit in with my short-, medium- or long-term strategy? By following the advice throughout this book you'll be able to make your goals a reality.

PART 1

REDUCING DEBT

One of the most vital things we need to do to become financially successful is reduce our debt load. When I started interviewing experts and successful Canadians, I was told that some financial advisors claim they know the "secrets to success." In truth, there really are no secrets.

Throughout history there have been people who have understood the core values of saving, paying down debt and investing. Benjamin Franklin was one of those people. I know you're saying, "Whoa, Pat, why are you talking about some guy who has been dead for 200 years? I want to save money in 2006!" Well, in 1757, Ben Franklin wrote a 3,500-word essay under the pseudonym Richard Saunders entitled *The Way to Wealth*. Even though almost 250 years have passed, many of the things that Franklin said then hold true today.

On overspending, Franklin said that "what maintains one vice, would bring up two children" and that even "a small leak will sink a great ship." He felt it was foolish to spend money on expensive clothing, saying, "Silks and satins, scarlet and velvets put out the kitchen fire" and that we should all wear our old coat a little longer. "

He knew of the desperation that people feel when they are deep in debt. "Poverty often deprives a man of all spirit and virtue. 'Tis hard for an empty bag to stand upright."

Franklin advised not to borrow as "the borrower is a slave to the lender ... ; be industrious and free; be frugal and free."

I know that time has passed and we now live in a much different world than Ben Franklin did, but many of his observations remain relevant today. It is nearly impossible not to be a borrower in this day and age, but in the following chapters we will look at some of the problems we face dealing with debt, such as debt consolidation, good debt versus bad debt and why your credit score is so important. Once you rid yourself of unnecessary debt you will feel more secure, at peace and confident in your future. As Franklin said, "a ploughman on his legs is higher than a gentleman on his knees."

attending credit counselling

If anyone has their finger on the pulse of consumer overspending, it is the front-line worker at credit counselling services across the country. They are the ones seeing the hundreds of thousands of consumers coming in, looking for a way to get out of the debt hole that they have dug themselves into. The Credit Counselling Service of Toronto is a non-profit organization that has helped more than 53,000 debt-ridden consumers in 2004 by phone and in person. Those numbers were up again in 2005 and debt loads were also much higher.

Project manager Laurie Campbell says what is happening in Canada's largest city is happening in equal measure from coast to coast. "There is no doubt about it. Savings rates are in a negative for the first time ever in Canadian history. Debt loads are at a record high, as well." Debt as a percentage of an average household's disposable income hit 122% in 2004. That is double the 61% level in 1961. Simply put, people are now spending significantly more than they make. Campbell says, "I don't know how people are going to get out of this. What it means is that people are even borrowing to pay debt. There is just no way they are able to finance their debt with the income they have."

The number one reason consumers finally seek credit counselling is credit cards. "It's as simple as that. It tells us it's unsecured debt, high-interest debt and debt that could have been avoided. It's usually because of impulsive spending, because one thing we know with credit cards is that it is very easy to spend impulsively," says Campbell.

As the consumer reporter for CTV I know all too well about the number of new consumer goods that come onto the market every week to encourage impulsive spending. Just when you think a product can't be made any differently, some company finds a way to make it new and improved. People want the best BBQs, televisions and computers. It's really not necessary and yet it's one way that people spend a huge chunk of their disposable income. Campbell says, "There is nothing wrong with buying the best product. It's just that consumers are not planning ahead. The biggest problem I see is that people have no goals that are specific enough for them to save money for. If they see a new gadget for their home on TV, they want to run out the next day and buy it. They are not looking at the larger picture because everyone needs short-term goals, intermediate goals and long-term goals. If people can have goals and stick to them, then they have a reason to save money and a reason to curb debt."

Just wanting to make changes and get out of debt is not enough. It's hard work and it's easier said than done. Whether you're trying to pay off $3,000 on one credit card or owe $35,000 in consolidation loans, student loans and credit card debt, you have to make serious lifestyle changes. "There is no magic solution. It takes a long time to get into debt and it's going to take a long time to get out of it. Changing lifestyle habits may mean not buying three or four coffees a day, not eating out all the time or not shopping at the mall for frivolous items every week. People have to really rethink where and how they spend their money."

Campbell encourages you to review your bank account monthly to see if your savings and equity are going up and your debt rate is going down. Some serious red flags are being waved at you if you're in constant worry about how bills will be paid, you're afraid to open your mail, you're getting calls from collection agencies, you're behind on rent or mortgage payments, you're using one credit card to pay for another or you're using credit for minor everyday expenses. I was once behind someone at a McDonald's who was using a credit card to buy a Big Mac. If you've reached that level, it's definitely time to reassess your finances. If you need help, credit counselling is a free, confidential place to get it.

Campbell says there is no need to be ashamed or embarrassed about your situation. "Basically we try to look at the whole financial picture. We look at everything—their income, their assets, their expenses and their debt—and we try to figure out the best possible way to resolve their financial problems. It may be consolidation loans or working with creditors to get the interest stopped and reduce payments," says Campbell.

A credit counselling consultation alone won't appear on your credit report, and that's what 85% of clients do—they go to get advice. The advice may be to make lifestyle changes, such as downsizing from an expensive apartment, getting a roommate, reducing their expenses or taking a part-time job to generate extra income.

If it's a more serious situation, counsellors may suggest a debt repayment program. They can also ask creditors to stop interest from accumulating and reduce payments. If you do go on a debt repayment program it will go on your credit record and remain there for up to two years after you have paid back your debt.

If it is an extremely serious situation, a "consumer proposal" may be necessary. This is someone saying to creditors, "I can't pay you back 100% but I can pay you 30%." This is based on a number of factors within the debtor's financial picture and at least it's not a bankruptcy. (I'll have more on bankruptcy in an upcoming chapter.)

Campbell, who sees new debt-laden consumers coming through her door every day, tries to be optimistic, but has grave concerns. She says, "I hate to be doom and gloom but I really can't see that this is going to be an easy situation for many people to get out of. I can see this turning into a crisis for many Canadians because there are so many people in debt. And it's not just a little bit of debt. It's large debt. So if interest rates start to spike and home prices fall we could see some real problems."

Non-profit, charitable credit counselling is available right across Canada. (There may be a small fee based on ability to pay for some debt management programs, but the interest relief is so much greater that it's well worth it.) You can get more information by calling 1-800-267-2272 or checking the website, www.creditcounsellingcanada.ca. Be aware that while debt consolidation can help, it's not a cure-all for debt woes. I'll tell you why in our next chapter.

consolidating debt

Like many people, I have consolidated debt in the past and have seen the wisdom of piling together several debts into one loan to get a lower interest rate. It's a no-brainer, right? Well, not really, and here's why.

Consolidating debt often just allows people to dig themselves further into debt. Those who constantly roll their debt into new loans never deal with the problem that is causing the consolidating in the first place—overspending! If you shuffle debt from one card to another or from a loan to a line of credit you will never get ahead, period. Consolidating various high interest rate balances into one, easy-to-handle payment is often just a quick fix to roll your "junk debt" into a bigger pile. What is "junk debt?" It's what I call debt that has been rolled around so many times you can't remember what you originally went into debt to buy in the first place.

Studies have shown that more than half of consumers who consolidate credit card debt have equal or higher amounts of credit card debt within two years. No wonder banks and credit card companies make it so easy for you to consolidate. Remember, just because a banker will approve a consolidation loan for the maximum amount you qualify for doesn't mean you should accept it.

And low-rate introductory credit card offers that allow you to transfer balances to take advantage of lower rates usually have time limits that make your savings minimal. *Lenders aren't in the charity business. They are trying to reel in another spender so they can make money off them for years.* Also, before you consider consolidation loans from those companies that advertise in the newspaper classifieds (the ones with rates akin to those of loan sharks), you really need to speak with a credit counsellor to assess just how deep a debt hole you are in.

Here's an example of junk debt in action. If you are like many people you have probably bought a pizza on a credit card. No big deal, right? It's just a pizza. Well, let's say you bought a pizza deal worth about $30 (maybe you got them to include some chicken wings) and you charged it to your credit card. You don't pay off your balance at the end of the month and you actually have an ongoing balance of about $1,500. Your credit card has an interest rate of 19%, so after a year you have paid $5.70 interest on your pizza. Still no big deal, right? Maybe it was really great pizza. You continue to pay minimum payments on your credit card and drag the balance through to another year. At this point, you still haven't paid for your pizza and now you're paying interest on the interest. Your pizza has cost you the original $30 + $5.70 in interest + another $6.78 in interest for a total of $42.48 so far, and you still haven't paid for it.

You eventually decide you shouldn't be paying such high interest on your credit card balance and take out a consolidation loan at the bank. With a lower interest rate, you are going to be saving money on your debt, or so you think.

And while you were getting a consolidation loan, you added in some debt from a couple of other credit cards, what was left of a car loan and a borrowed couple of grand for a trip to Florida. Well, this consolidation loan is for 10% over four years. This means the yearly interest on your pizza is now $4.25 a year over four years, so $42.48 + $4.25 + $4.25 + $4.25 + $4.25 = $59.48. You digested that pizza long ago *but you still haven't paid for it!*

If you are like many consumers with a home, you may be convinced by a banker to take out a line of credit to get an even lower interest rate. At some point throughout the period of the consolidation loan, you decide to lump it into that line of credit with home renovations or a new car at an interest rate of just 6%. Great, or is it? Now that you have an interest rate of 6%, you are likely to just make the minimum monthly interest payments because you think it's such a terrific deal and you've racked up debt elsewhere that you have to pay off as well. So every year you pay 6% on your line of credit, paying off little of the original balance. This could go on for years, paying 6% on that pizza one year, 6% the next, 6% the year after that and so on and so on. I hope that pizza tasted good, because it will end up costing you hundreds of dollars.

This calculation makes the point that consolidating debt just means it will take you longer to pay it off. Consolidating is a short-term solution that in the long run costs you plenty. The example could also have been of a CD that wasn't very good anyway and you only listened to it three times, a sweater you wore twice or a night on the town that you would rather forget.

Having said all this, if you are truly ready to turn your financial life around and put your nose to the debt reduction grindstone, then debt consolidation can be a good thing. Just be mindful the odds are against you and the banks are counting on you to run up your credit cards again so you will be back to consolidate again in the future. As for me, I like pizza as much as the next person, but now I only pay cash for it.

curbing bad spending habits

It's hard to get ahead if you have bad habits eating away at your bank account. The obvious ones that come to mind are the vices of smoking and excessive alcohol consumption. Neither is good for your physical nor financial health. A pack of smokes a day at $8 a pack equals $2,920 a year. And that is after-tax spending, so you would need to earn about $4,500 to keep yourself puffing for 365 days. A friend of mine and his wife, both lifelong smokers, were finally able to butt out. They wanted to quit for health reasons, but the final straw was when they calculated their bad habit was costing their family about $10,000 a year. A case of 24 bottles of premium Canadian lager at $35 a weekend is $1,820 annually. The cost is about the same cost if you buy just two bottles of fancy wine every week. No one is suggesting you give up your glass of wine but everyone should be aware that expensive wine, jewellery and movie collections can make saving money nearly impossible.

Author David Bach coined the phrase "The Latte Factor," meaning the little expenses can really add up. A $4 a day latte habit can add up to $1,460 over a year. In Canada it could be called the "The Tim Hortons Factor," as we all know someone who can't start their day without a Tim Hortons coffee. (People actually call me at

CTV, wanting to know if there is a drug in Tim Hortons coffee that keeps them going back. "Yes," I tell them. "It's called caffeine.") Now, you may not want to cut out your morning coffee if it really is an important part of your daily routine, but you may be surprised at how much you're spending. When I asked a family to monitor their spending over a week's time for a segment I was doing for *Canada AM*, they were amazed to see that over a year they would spend more than $1,500 at the local coffee shop. They decided not to cut out their morning coffee completely, but to at least cut back.

Collecting CDs can really add up. When I was younger, I would buy one or two CDs a week. They were 20 bucks each back then. Even buying one CD a week adds up to more than $1,000 a year. I curtailed my CD spending long ago and have to admit there are only about 20 in my large collection that I listen to with any regularity now.

The hot new trend these days is people buying DVDs and having huge DVD collections. How many times do you really need to watch a movie? Sure, movies for the kids make sense, and if you are a *Lord of the Rings* or *The Godfather* series fanatic then you might want to pick them up to have, but starting a DVD collection is an expensive proposition. I was behind someone at a store recently and he was buying three DVDs for $75. If that's something he does often, that kind of spending will add up fast. I know someone with a massive DVD collection. He takes the bus because he can't afford a car, but he does have every episode of *The Twilight Zone*.

Another expensive habit is eating out. I'm the first to admit I hate packing a lunch. I've tried and failed at brown-bagging it. The truth is I don't mind spending $5 to $7 a day to eat lunch. I am often in different locations doing interviews, or live hits as we say in the business, so it really is much easier for me to grab something on the go. It's when I dine with big spenders who want to do the sit-down lunch thing, complete with appetizers and desserts, that lunch-time spending can get out of control. Of course, there is nothing wrong with dining out occasionally, whether it's for lunch or for dinner. But when people make it normal practice to spend $25 or more for lunch it becomes reckless spending. I knew a couple who ate out every Friday night at an upscale restaurant, spending at least $100 a week. That's $5,200 a year! They did it to reward themselves and said it helped their marriage, but they eventually divorced. I don't think the expensive meals made much of a difference in the end.

This can also be said of buying expensive clothing or furniture. I know of parents who keep themselves in debt just so their children can wear the latest fashions to school. Talk about teaching kids to keep up with the Joneses at a young age. The same is true of people who buy expensive clothing for themselves. There is nothing wrong with having a good wardrobe, especially if you can afford it, but spending thousands of dollars a year being a clotheshorse is wasteful and unnecessary. And again, the same is true of furniture. Once you buy one high-end piece you will feel compelled to surround it with similar pieces. I know someone who bought an expensive, imported, custom-made leather couch and then felt he had to complement it with other high-end furniture that cost him a fortune. He is still renting an apartment. (It has nice furniture, though.)

Going to the movies is another area where costs can really add up. I did a story that calculated how much it would cost for a family of four to see just two movies a month over the course of a year—with popcorn and drinks, of course.

Tickets for a family of four	=	$37
Popcorn and drinks	=	$26
Total	=	$63
Two movies a month for 12 months	=	$1,512

Hard to believe that going to the movies a couple of times a month would cost more than $1,500 a year.

And then there's golf. I know people that golf three to four times a week. Golfing twice a week at a course that costs $50 to play 18 holes, which is not uncommon, adds up to $100 a week, $400 a month and $2,400 a season.

Another area of concern is gambling. People, especially young people, are visiting casinos and spending hundreds of dollars on each visit. People are blowing a lot of money and the government knows it's a huge problem. More about this later in the book.

Ten Common Money Wasters

Dining out often at restaurants

Buying expensive clothing and jewellery

Using premium gasoline (if your car doesn't require it; most don't)

Dry cleaning clothes you could wash yourself

Buying a brand new car

Using name-brand products when generics will do

Flying first class

Running up excessive cell and phone bills

Purchasing extended warranty plans

Buying DVDs, CDs and computer games

I think the point to be made is that there is nothing wrong with having nice clothes, a beautiful dining set, seeing the occasional movie or eating out. The key is *"can you afford it?"* If you can, great. It's when bad lifestyle habits develop that drain your finances and make it impossible to get ahead that you should be concerned. Old habits die hard, but as Benjamin Franklin said, "What maintains one vice, would bring up two children." Now may be a good time to review your spending habits to ensure you're not being wasteful.

differentiating good debt from bad debt

I had a boss who once told me, "You can make far more money in a day with your head than you can with your hands." It's true, and many wealthy Canadians have done it by knowing the difference between good debt and bad debt and by using the power of "leverage." In speaking with money managers who work with millionaires, I found out that understanding leverage as a wealth-building tool is the single most effective way that the rich become wealthy. Leveraging is also known as "using other people's money."

Good debt produces cash flow; bad debt doesn't. Bad debt is a loan for a depreciating asset (such as a car, a boat or a trip to Florida) while good debt is something that will grow in value (such as your home, an income property or a business). Clothing purchased on a credit card is bad debt. Getting a loan to buy a three-unit apartment building is good debt (usually). Borrowing money to go to school, take a professional training course or make an investment in yourself can also be considered good debt. Bad debt comes from the endless temptation of vacations, dining out, movies, gifts, golf or other entertainment.

Now of course, we all need to have some fun, but if you want to get serious about your finances follow this basic rule: *If you are going to buy something that doesn't go up in value you should pay cash for it.* This can be difficult when buying a car, which is why you should never purchase a brand new, expensive car when you are still in the process of paying down debt. (We will deal later on with cars and why buying brand new is a waste of money.)

Leverage and recognizing the difference between good debt and bad debt is one way that the rich people of Canada become richer. Not knowing the difference is what keeps poor people poor.

Most people have their first experience with leverage and good debt when they buy their first home. You borrow money to buy a house, it appreciates in value and you get to live in it—it's a winning combination. For example, let's look at a buyer who has $25,000 to put down on a $275,000 home. If that home rises in price to $300,000 then that buyer has effectively doubled their money—they have turned $25,000 into $50,000! Over time, if the home rises $100,000 in value, then the buyer has turned his initial $25,000 into $100,000! This is the power of leverage—using the bank's money to increase your bottom line. At the same time you will be paying down your mortgage on your home and seeing your net worth increase.

The power of leverage, combined with saving and paying down debt, can give you an astounding return on your money. Leverage can also go both ways, which is why you could also open yourself up to greater losses. For example, taking $100,000 of equity out of your home to buy a condo could be a good investment. However, if you purchase a bad unit, the real estate market takes a downturn, you end up with a bad tenant or your maintenance fees double, you could be in a worse position. Leveraging must be used with caution and respect.

The next most common form of leveraging is borrowing to invest. Whether it's a line of credit or bank loan, the interest on money borrowed to invest is tax deductible, which is an added benefit. Often you can just pay the interest from month to month, never paying down the principal. The goal, of course, is to turn your $50,000 loan into $100,000 and then $200,000 and so on.

Leveraging and using other people's money and knowing the difference between good debt and bad debt will help you achieve wealth much faster than saving alone.

establishing an emergency fund

It's amazing how many families have joint incomes of $80,000 but still can't write out a cheque for $500 on the spur of the moment without it becoming an exercise in juggling accounts, using a bank overdraft or taking a cash advance on their credit card. Do you occasionally have to cross your fingers when you hand a clerk your credit or debit card, hoping there will be enough there to cover your purchase? When we don't have enough money set aside to cover an emergency like a refrigerator repair, a furnace breakdown or a new water pump for the car, we can find ourselves desperate and making rash decisions. We may have to use credit and pile on more debt or end up in a financing deal that will cost much more than if we had the cash at the ready to make the purchase or pay the bills. What if your company closed down, went on strike or you lost your job? What if you had to make an emergency overseas trip to see a sick relative? Having money set aside for emergencies is diffi-cult to do, but it must become part of your total financial strategy.

We are told by financial experts that we should have three to six months' salary saved up in case we lose our job or have an unforeseen emergency, but the truth is most of us don't. I'm the first to admit that I don't have a half a year's salary in my savings account (and with the interest most banks pay for savings, there are better places to keep your money). However, I could liquidate stocks and mutual funds (outside my RRSP) if I needed a large amount of money in a hurry. Hopefully I won't have to and you won't either.

The problem with emergency funds is that people seem to struggle with exactly what an emergency is. A sale on big screen TVs is not an emergency, nor is an opportunity for a last-minute trip to Vegas with your friends. It's that whole "want or need" thing. It's human nature to want to spend easily accessible money. That's one drawback to having a big pile of easily accessible cash. The emergency fund is a true test of your willpower and discipline.

Home equity loans, cash advances on credit cards, and bank overdrafts are not emergency funds. If you are strapped for cash and your backup plan is to dig yourself further into debt using more credit, then you obviously don't have an emergency fund at all. Definitely try to have *at least* $1,000 to $2,000 in readily accessible cash in the bank so you will not be forced to turn to credit when the inevitable emergency arises. The money should be easily accessible in your bank account, but depending on your willpower it may need to be set aside in a separate account from your debit and chequing accounts so you won't consider a Friday night Chinese food craving an emergency. I would also argue that having a large amount of money sitting in a savings account earning 2% or having $50 and $100 bills crammed under your mattress earning you nothing is not the best emergency fund.

> If you dip into your emergency fund for an unexpected legitimate expense, top it back up as soon as you can so the fund will be ready for the next "rainy day" when an emergency comes knocking.

If you're considering stocks, bonds or mutual funds as the source of your emergency fund, consider holding them outside your RRSP. Too many people have savings within their RRSPs but little invested outside of them. Anyone who has ever faced a cash crunch and withdrew money from their retirement savings can tell you what a massive tax hit they took. Remember the cash you got back on your income tax when you put money in your RRSP? Well, if you ever pull money out of your RRSP, the federal government will want back the tax money it gave you as an incentive to save. Depending on your tax bracket, you could remove $10,000 and have to pay back $4,000 in tax. The moral: never count on using your RRSP as an emergency fund—it will cost you big time.

Your rainy day fund will come in handy when your car battery dies or your furnace quits. You'll be glad you have it when that time comes.

hopping from credit card to credit card

Are you the type of consumer who jumps from one credit card to the next, trying to maintain a low interest rate on your debt? If so, the British would call you a "rate tart." In our credit crazy society where we don't pay a cent, put no money down, and have no payments for six months it's increasingly easy to buy now and pay later. Of course, if you borrow from Peter to pay Paul long enough, eventually Peter wants his money back. That's when the credit card hopping can begin! Credit card companies sure make it easy by sending 0% interest introductory offers to your door every other week. Of course, the low rates are for a limited time and there are many strings attached, so credit card hopping can easily lead you to leap into a huge pile of debt.

Laurie Campbell with the Credit Counselling Service of Toronto says credit card hopping is increasingly common and has become the latest band-aid solution for consumers who have lost control of their spending. Campbell says, "People who come to us for help will have several high-interest-rate credit cards and are hopping around trying to get a lower interest rate. The problem is they continue using their original credit cards so in the end they have a low-interest-rate card with a balance, plus other cards with balances as well. Instead of being better off they are actually further behind."

Credit card hoppers have to come to terms with why they are ending up with huge balances in the first place. New statistics offer startling insight into just how much debt the average person is in. "Canadians are using 100% of their disposable income to service debt," notes Campbell. Canadians are getting further and further in debt every year and the ability to service this debt will be impossible for many over time."

Fueling the credit-card hopping trend is the number of American credit companies that have come into Canada to set up shop and reel in new customers. They send out tens of thousands of applications every week with low introductory interest rate offers. If the mailing comes at a time of the month when a consumer is feeling particularly bombarded by bills they may decide to sign up. As Campbell says, "If you throw a bowling ball down the lane, chances are you are going to hit a couple of pins." The low introductory rates do allow consumers to transfer the balances from a high-interest card to a low-interest one. Many consumers are optimistic their situation will improve and that they will be able to get out of debt before the low rates expire. However, if they don't change their spending habits, there is little chance they will get ahead.

Compounding the problem is that credit card agreements are not the same as they were five years ago. The fine print on credit card statements now comes with new rules, such as late fee charges, over-balance charges and higher interest rates if you miss a payment. Just missing a payment by one day could cause your low introductory rate of 0% to jump to 18% or more. The same is true for "convenience credit cheques," which also encourage spending and have hidden fees. Another catch that many consumers are unaware of is that while you may be paying a reduced rate of interest on transferred balances, new purchases or already existing balances will be charged at the higher rate, and the amount of money you pay each month will go to service the low-interest-rate debt while the high-interest-rate debt piles up. Just one shopping spree could leave you deeper in trouble. Campbell says, "People think the interest rate is really low so I'll go and buy some things that I only thought about buying, but couldn't afford. Well, guess what? They still can't afford them."

Of course, it's always a good idea to get the lowest interest rate possible, so if you are serious about reducing your debt load then accepting a low rate credit card offer can be a good strategy. It's estimated that one of three people who transfer their balances from cards with higher interest rates have success at reducing their debt load.

The key to success with credit-card hopping is closing credit card accounts as soon as the balances are transferred from them. It's when credit card accounts are left open that you run into problems! Many people decide to keep the credit cards active in case of an emergency. This might make sense for a true emergency, but too often "emergencies" become a sale on a digital camera or a night on the town after a stressful day at work. As mentioned in the previous chapter, if you have an emergency fund you won't need to pay on credit for a new radiator for your car or plumber for your stopped-up kitchen sink.

Do be aware that every time you apply for credit it shows up on your credit rating. If you are hopping from one credit card to another and opening and closing accounts, these activities will show up on your credit file and lower your credit score. It can look like you are a credit junkie or someone who has been denied credit all over town so you are searching for it wherever you can. If you have many accounts open, then a lender may also feel your abundance of credit could also quickly turn into an abundance of debt. Either way, credit hopping will negatively affect your credit rating.

So how much can you save with a low rate offer? Here's an example. If you had credit card debt of $5,000 and you were making the minimum monthly payments, this is how much you would save if you switched from a card with an 18% interest rate to one with an interest rate of 8.9%.

Credit Card Debt of $5,000

Paying 5% minimum payments
New balances after six months

18% interest	8.9% interest
$4,037.00	$3,851.02

Savings: $185.98

If you were making minimum monthly payments you would have saved $185.98 after six months. A savings of $185.98 is not a huge amount, but if you did not add to your debt during this period it would definitely be considered a success. If you are really serious about paying off your debt then you want to pay more than your minimum monthly payment. For example:

Credit Card Debt of $5,000 at 18% Interest

Paying 5% minimum payment	Paying $250 fixed payment
Debt free in 115 months!	Debt free in 24 months!
$2,096.70 in interest charges	$989.13 in interest charges

By cracking down and paying a flat amount of $250 a month, not only would you save more than $1,100 in interest charges, the debt would be wiped out in two years instead of more than nine! Imagine having that debt hanging over your head for nine years.

An excellent debit calculator is offered through www.credit-canada.com. The website can show you just how long it will take to pay off your debt and how much interest your behaviour will cost you.

The bottom line? You need a plan of action to pay off debt. Whether you are paying 6%, 18% or 24% interest, it's still too much—you want to eliminate it. If you are serious about paying down your debt then taking advantage of a low-rate credit card to transfer your balances from high-rate cards is a good idea. But if you fall into a credit-card-hopping scenario or, as the Brits say, become a "rate tart," then these offers should be shredded as soon as they arrive in your mailbox. The golden rule: If credit is a problem, then one credit card is all you should have. Being a rate tart will reflect badly on your credit score, and as you will see in a few chapters, your credit score is one of the most important signs of financial health you have.

bidding farewell to your credit cards

If you have several credit cards with debt you should set goals to pay them off one at a time. Start with the highest interest rate card first. If you have a department store card at 28% you should pay as much money as you can on it every month until you get the balance to zero. If you have other credit cards, make minimum payments on them, but stick to paying off that 28% card first. When you get that credit card to zero, call the department store's finance department and cancel the card. Then get to work on your next credit card.

The problem with credit cards that you pay off is that they are like vampires that want to live another day. Here are four good reasons why you should chop up your paid-off cards and call the lenders to close the accounts.

1. You can buckle down and get the balance to zero, but if you don't drive a stake through them they are there, ready to rise again and rack up debt!
2. If you got the balance to zero by getting a consolidation loan or line of credit to pay it off, you may think your should keep the credit card around just in case, for possible emergencies. But if you haven't dealt with your free-spending ways and have a period of weakness, you will run up the card again.

Then you are left with a consolidation loan and credit cards once again loaded with debt!

3. Whatever the credit limit is on the card, that limit is considered potential debt by lenders. After all, if you don't cancel the card, it will remain open on your credit file and a card that has not been canceled is just waiting and ready in your wallet or purse to go on a spending spree.

4. Every card you have will lower your credit score (a very important number I'll tell you about more in the next chapter). After I did a story on how to check your credit score, a very upset woman contacted me. "What is the problem?" I asked. She could not figure out why she had such a low credit score. She had few debts, no loans and always paid her bills on time. After some discussion it became clear what she did have was a purse full of credit cards—about 15 in all! Whenever a credit card company sent her an application, she filled it out. She had all the major credit cards, gas cards, department store cards, etc. Even though she did not have balances on most of them, as far as the credit reporting agency was concerned she had credit limits totaling about $100,000, and if she wanted to go on a $100,000 spending spree she could. I advised her to keep one or two cards, cut the rest up and *close every account to let the cards rest in peace!*

This is why once you have paid off a credit card you must let it rest in peace! You have to call your credit card company and say, "I have paid off my account and I am done with your company. Please cancel my credit card." Too many consumers mistakenly believe that once they have paid off a card and cut it up, it's over. Done. Kaput. That is not the case.

Be careful because credit card companies will send you new applications or even new credit cards periodically, hoping to catch you in a weak spot when you may need a credit fix. Don't fall for it. Credit cards are like a bad relationship that should be ended.

obtaining your credit score and credit report

Big brother is watching you in the form of Equifax and TransUnion, Canada's two major credit agencies. They know every time you sign up for a loan, lease a car or get a department store charge card.

Did you know there is a magic number they assign to you that banks and lenders look at before they loan you money or approve a credit card? Many of us have heard the term "credit rating" but the proper term for this number is actually "credit score." Until recently, this score was kept a secret from you, but now for a fee you can see how you rate as a credit risk compared with other Canadians. Your credit score is a deciding factor on whether you will be approved for a mortgage, car loan or credit card. If you're a high risk, you'll pay a higher rate of interest or not be accepted at all. This is not the same as your credit report; you've always been able to get that for free and I will tell you how you can do that in a moment. Your credit score is a mathematical calculation known as a FICO score that uses information in your credit history to determine the likelihood of whether or not you'll skip out on a car loan or miss a mortgage payment.

FICO stands for Fair Isaac Company, the organization that developed the scoring mechanism for the credit score. This score is what will be used by companies to determine whether you are a safe financial risk or not. In order to even have a FICO score, you must have at least one open account on your credit report and that account needs to have been open for at least six months.

Your credit score is made up of a number of factors and you are judged on a sliding scale between 900 and 300. The higher your number, the better you are as a credit risk. Most people don't know their FICO score, but you should because if you have a high score (the favourable end of the chart) you can use it to your advantage to try to get lower interest rates on loans. It doesn't hurt to find out if you have a low score either, because then you can work to improve it. Here is an example of a FICO score from Equifax Canada.

FICO® Score 760
For: Louise Guidry

- Your FICO score of **760** summarizes the information on your Equifax credit report.
- FICO scores range between **300** and **900**.
- Higher scores are considered better scores. That is, the higher your score, the more favourably lenders look upon you as a credit risk.
- Your score is slightly below the average score of Canadian consumers, though most lenders consider this a good score.

Figure 18.1: The Bottom Line: What a FICO score of 760 means to you.

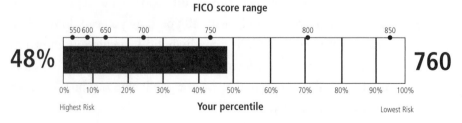

Adapted from illustration courtesy of Equifax Canada.

So why did Louise get a FICO score of 760? Credit agencies judge credit scores based on the following criteria:

- 35% of your score is based on your payment history. Have you paid your bills on time? How many have been paid late? Have you ever had a collection agency after you? Have you ever declared bankruptcy? How long ago these things happened will also affect your score. Something that happened six years ago will not impact your score as negatively as if you skipped a bill last month.

- 30% of your credit score is based on your outstanding debt. Are you swamped with debt already and have little room left to pay your bills? How much do you owe on your home and your car? How many credit cards do you have and are they at their limits? The more credit cards you have, again, the lower your score.

- 15% of your score is based on how long you have had credit. The longer, the better. Your past payment history can help predict how you'll pay your bills in the future.

- 10% of your score is based on the number of inquiries on your report. If you check on your own that's not a problem. However, if there have been a number of inquiries from potential creditors, it's possibly an indication that you've been all over town trying to get credit and have been turned down, so this will reflect poorly and lower your credit score. It could indicate you have too much debt or too many credit cards. Usually only inquiries from the past year are counted.

- 10% of the score is based on the type of credit you already have—the number of charge cards you have along with outstanding loans. There is no perfect number that you should or shouldn't have, but this will be more closely scrutinized if there isn't an abundance of other information on your credit file.

So how do Canadians rate? The vast majority of us, about 70%, have credit scores between 700 and 850, which is an acceptable range to be in. Someone like Louise, with a credit score of 760, for example, would be considered a good credit risk.

Figure 18.2: National Distribution of FICO Scores

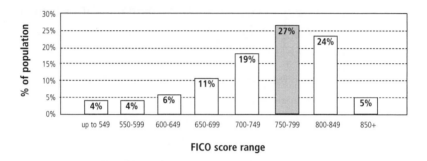

Adapted from illustration courtesy of Equifax Canada.

The delinquency rate for someone in the 750 to 799 range is 2%, meaning that for every 100 borrowers in this category, approximately two will default on a loan, file for bankruptcy or fail to make a payment for three months. Still, in the lending business these are considered good odds and a very acceptable risk, so it's highly unlikely you would be turned down for a credit card or loan. Most lenders would consider offering you attractive interest rates and provide you with near instant approval.

If your credit score is higher than 850, you are in the top 5% of the country with a select group of consumers who have an impeccable credit rating. If you are below 700, your credit rating is on shakier ground. If you are below 600, you may be turned down for loans and credit cards and should start working to turn around your credit score. The lowest category, which has credit scores between 300 and 500, has delinquency rates of 78%! Anyone in this zone will have a tough time getting credit of any kind. See the Appendix for Equifax Canada's "Summary of factors affecting your score."

One of the best ways to improve your credit score is to stop borrowing money! Only apply for credit when you really need it. Avoid signing up for new credit cards and maxing out the ones you already have.

Your Credit Report

Every major financial transaction involving a lender is kept on file with Equifax and TransUnion and every time you're late paying a bill it's a black mark on your record. Your credit report also tells lenders if you have ever declared bankruptcy or co-signed for a loan, as well as your personal information, such as date of birth, addresses, employment information, creditors, payment history and inquiries that have been made into your credit history. *You should know that all credit information, good or bad, is kept on file for six years (some provinces could keep it as long as seven years and Prince Edward Island keeps bankruptcies on file for 14 years). Information like failing to pay a credit card bill for several months will come off at the end of the six years in a systematic purge. That's why if you have had bad credit in the past there is hope to get your score back in shape.*

Obtaining Your Score and Report

By going online at www.equifax.ca *or* www.transunion.ca *and paying $25 including tax, you can obtain both your credit score and credit report (this is the only way to obtain your credit score).* Because of the cost, I would not recommend that you check your credit score often; however, I would check it once and print off the paperwork along with your credit report for your files. This way you can make sure everything is in order and you can work to improve your score. You may wish to check your score again in a year or two to see if it has improved. It doesn't hurt to check your credit score before you go to apply for a loan so you will not have any surprises when you are sitting across from the bank manager. Also, keep in mind that your ability to pay back a loan is also based on your income, so don't think with a good credit score you can borrow all the money you want!

If you have a low credit score you can and should work to improve it. First, review your credit report to make sure there are no mistakes. You can correct errors by contacting one of the credit reporting agencies. However, if the negative information is correct it will remain on your credit file. Second, close accounts you no longer use or need. Too often, people pay off credit cards and even cut them up but fail to close the account with the lender. An active credit card account can hamper your ability to get new credit. Third, you should reduce your balances on cards to less than 75% of your available credit (30% is preferable). Fourth, the most important consideration is to pay your bills on time! This cannot be stressed enough. Finally, don't let anyone make an inquiry about your credit score unless they absolutely have to, as repeated inquiries can lower your score. Doing these things will not have an immediate impact on your credit score because it takes time for your score to improve.

To get your credit report *free of charge*, you can call Equifax at 1-800-465-7166 or write them at Equifax Canada Inc., Consumer Relations Department, Box 190 Jean Talon Station, Montreal, Quebec, H1S 2Z2. You can also call TransUnion at 1-800-663-9980 or write them at 170 Jackson Street East, Hamilton, Ontario, L8N 3K8. It will take 10 to 15 days before you get your credit report in the mail. When sending in for your credit file you should include your name, including any maiden name, daytime and evening phone numbers, your current address and previous address (if you've moved in the past few years), your date of birth and marital status. Include your social insurance number and photocopies of two pieces of identification, such as a driver's licence or credit card. TransUnion also requires a photocopy of a utility bill. If you are requesting credit information for your spouse, then include their name, social insurance number and identification as well.

When you receive your credit report, it will have a list of the lenders you have dealt with, the type of loans, balances, credit limits, date of last activity, and the number of times you have been 30, 60 or 90 days late making a payment. It will have information about bankruptcies, judgments and collection agencies. It will also list the number of times companies have requested a copy of your credit report. It will also tell you "soft" inquiries, which are when lenders look at your file. These soft inquires are displayed to you but do not affect your credit.

If you have never checked your credit score or credit report before, I would highly recommend you start. You can then see where you rate compared with other Canadians. Again, don't check this often; once a year at the most. Checking your score regularly will let you know if your FICO score is improving, if your credit report is mistake free and also if you have been the victim of identity fraud—something I will address later in this book. *Your credit score and credit report are two of the most important financial tools you have, so treat them like gold.*

dealing with collection agencies

If you start missing loan payments or paying your credit card bills late, chances are you have a debt problem and you may one day find a collection agency knocking at your door. Having an account sent to a collection agency can have dire consequences and put a black mark on your credit report that can be difficult to get off. You should do everything possible to avoid having a debt go to collections. If you have defaulted on your financial obligations don't panic; try to deal directly with the company you owe money to. If you can't make a payment, tell them why and when you hope to be able to be caught up on your accounts. This will show them you are serious about paying the money back. If your bills pile up too much and you have no way of getting ahead of the debt you have created, you may find that the company will send your account to collections rather than deal with you.

Dealing with a collection agency can be a frustrating and stressful experience, but you must remember that it is simply an organization arranging repayment for the money that you owe. Here are some tips for dealing with collection agencies.

- Be civil and realize the collection agency's involvement is nothing personal. Once your account is paid in full you won't have to deal with them again.

- Once a collection agency is involved, deal directly with them. There is no need to contact the original business unless there is an error. If there is a mistake or you dispute the amount owed, advise the collection agency and the creditor immediately and do your best to provide documents to back up your case.

- If possible, try to settle the account and pay the money immediately. If you can't, and for many people it isn't possible as this is the reason the collection agency is calling, try to arrange a schedule for repayment.

- Try to offer alternative methods of restitution, either in a lump sum or a series of monthly payments.

- Never pay off debts by sending cash. Instead, make payments in a way that you will have proof of payment. A receipt or canceled cheque can prevent arguments later.

- Once you make arrangements to pay off your debt, be sure not to miss payments or bounce cheques. If you do, you could end up in court, have your wages garnished, have your assets seized as well as receive a major blemish on your credit report that will haunt you for six years.

Because collection agencies are often promised a larger commission if they can get you to pay sooner, some can be quite aggressive. Regulations differ across the country but generally a collection agency cannot try to collect a debt without notifying you first in writing. Collection agencies cannot make harassing telephone calls or give false or misleading information that could damage your reputation. If you have been contacted by a collection agency and truly feel you don't owe anything to anyone or you believe you're are being treated unfairly, contact your provincial Ministry of Consumer and Commercial Relations to find out what options are available to you.

steering clear of payday loan services

Anyone caught in a financial crunch may feel the need to go to a payday loan or cash advance service. *Don't do it*! Borrowing from these guys will almost certainly ensure you'll never get ahead. Following complaints that many payday loan services were acting like loan sharks, moves are underway to rein in exorbitant insurance fees, administrative costs and interest charges.

It's a billion-dollar industry in Canada, with as many as 1,500 outlets and more opening all the time. Typically, consumers who find themselves short of cash use their paycheque as collateral to borrow several hundred dollars for a period of not more than two weeks. While some may feel a quick cash fix could help them over a financial "hump," unfortunately many clients of these services get caught in a debt spiral.

As banks vacate small towns and poorer urban areas, these high-interest-rate loan services are moving in, and there is concern they are exploiting the working poor. The federal government has announced plans to give the provinces new powers to crack down on the payday industry, and with the heat on there are positive changes taking effect that will help protect consumers.

The Canadian Payday Loan Association, a lobby group that represents about two-thirds of payday loan stores, now has "The Code of Best Business Practices," a voluntary code that it says will help protect consumers. One practice it has put an end to is "rollover loans," which allowed customers to take out a second loan to pay off the first one, resulting in compounded interest.

> Rollover loans create an endless cycle of loans with high interest charges and administrative fees that can leave some customers borrowing for years, unable to pay back the original amount they borrowed in the first place.

I have interviewed people who have been caught running from one payday lender to another, borrowing from Peter to pay Paul. One man told me his situation was so desperate that he owed more than $6,000 and was using 13 cash advance services at the same time before he finally attended credit counselling.

The Association of Community Organizations for Reform Now (ACORN) has been leading the charge on payday loan reforms. ACORN was the first organization in Canada to be vocal about how the payday industry was taking advantage of consumers and operating with few rules and regulations like it was in the Wild West. Its goal has been to lobby the government to make sure that consumers, especially low-income earners, are not paying outrageous interest payments for short-term loans. ACORN argues that interest rates charged by payday lenders should be criminal under Canadian law. According to section 347 of the Criminal Code, annual interest rates for loans must not exceed 60%.

ACORN calculates that cash advance services break the law everyday by routinely charging annual rates between 300% and 900% interest. ACORN argues that if, for example, someone were to borrow $400 for two weeks, with a lending fee charged of $51.84, this is an annual interest rate of 1,092%. ACORN wants interest rates capped and tighter restrictions placed on how payday loan services operate. The Canadian Payday Loan Association argues that comparing two-week loans to annual loans is like comparing weekly car rentals to car ownership. The industry claims payday lending allows Canadians to get small, short-term loans without having to turn to friends or family.

One thing is clear: if you or someone you know is using payday loan services often, then they have other financial problems that must be dealt with. If you have an emergency fund, can plan ahead and know how much money is flowing in and out of your life, you can avoid ever having to walk into a payday loan store. Don't let payday loan stores make money off you.

If you have a concern or a complaint about the payday loan industry, you can call toll-free 1-800-413-0147 or go online at www.cpla-acps.ca. All complaints will be investigated.

CHAPTER 21

declaring bankruptcy

You may think of someone who declares bankruptcy as a reckless spender on unemployment or welfare who is racking up bills they have no intention of paying back, but the truth is they are working steadily, have a good income and may look a lot like your next door neighbour or even you. The latest research finds that many consumers who turn to bankruptcy are middle class people in their 30s and 40s who are going through a life-changing event, such as a job loss, illness or divorce.

In Canada 2004 there were 110,940 total bankruptcies. Of this number, 101,084 were consumers while 9,856 were businesses. That's an average increase of 12.8 % every year since 1968.

Hoyes, Michalos and Associates performed a study in the fall of 2005 that found that the typical person declaring bankruptcy is an average Canadian living paycheque to paycheque. Douglas Hoyes, a bankruptcy trustee with the firm, says, "Many families that are overspending can squeak by paying the bills with two incomes, but as soon as one person loses a job or leaves the household, it's only a matter of weeks before the mounting bills become a serious problem."

Based on individuals and families they assisted over three years, the firm says its research found Canada's typical bankruptcy case to be someone they refer to as "Joe Debtor." Let's look at some of the data on who is going broke.

Gender of Insolvent Debtor	
Gender	Distribution
Male	54%
Female	46%

Age of Insolvent Debtor	
Age	Distribution
18–30	22%
31–40	31%
41–50	26%
51–60	15%
Over 60	6%

Marital Status of Insolvent Debtor	
Marital Status	Distribution
Married	37%
Single	32%
Separated	15%
Divorced	14%
Widowed	2%

The average Joe Debtor is ...

Gender: Male

Weighted average age: 40.5 years old

Total unsecured debt: $50,755

Likelihood they own a home: 20% (one in five clients are home owners)

Average mortgage value: $134,432

Average family size: two people (including the debtor)

Average monthly income: $2,419 net of deductions

And how is the $50,755 in unsecured debt that Joe Debtor owes split up?

- He owes major Canadian banks $30,645 including loans, lines of credit and credit cards.

- He owes other major credit cards $6,210.

- He owes Canada Revenue Agency $6,020 (51% of the firm's bankrupcies have debts with CRA; the average debt is $11,770 for those that do).

- He owes high-interest lenders $3,824 (50% of the firm's clients owe debts to high-interest lenders; the average debt is $7,694).

- He owes miscellaneous debtors $4,056.

The events that lead to bankruptcy are unfortunately quite predictable, and bankruptcy trustees see the same signs over and over again. Hoyes elaborates, saying, "You may be cruising through life and everything seems fine. You have a good job, you're married, you've bought a house, leased a car, bought some furniture on credit cards and taken out a line of credit. But if a life-changing event happens to you, then unfortunately many people are only one or two paycheques away from serious financial trouble." Here are the reasons that more than 100,000 Canadians went bankrupt last year.

Causes of Insolvency

Causes of Financial Difficulty	Rate
Over extension of credit, financial mismanagement	40%
Job related (unemployment, layoff, reduction in pay)	33%
Unable to service debt (low income, business failure, other reasons)	22%
Marital or relationship breakdown	16%
Illness, injury and health-related problems	16%

Numbers do not add to 100% since some debtors gave more than one cause for their insolvency.

If you recognize early enough the financial problems you have created for yourself, it is possible to change your situation and avoid bankruptcy. Hoyes says, "You can get a debt consolidation loan with the bank and dramatically cut your expenses so the final option of filing for bankruptcy isn't necessary, but you have got to take action fast because financial problems don't go away on their own."

The most important thing to do is to know exactly where your money is going. The role of a bankruptcy trustee is to show a cash-strapped consumer their true financial picture. "We sit down with people and help them make a list of everything they owe and put the interest rates beside it and that alone is a shock to most people. We then make a list of what it costs to live every month. When you see that you bring in $2,000 a month and it costs you $2,000 a month to service your debt, that pretty much is the wake-up call that you've got to do something drastic to change your situation."

If you have sought professional help from a debt counsellor or bankruptcy trustee and they feel that bankruptcy is the only way for you to get a fresh start and relieve your debt burden, you may have to consider filing for bankruptcy.

When Bankruptcy Is the Only Way Out

Declaring bankruptcy is not a decision to be made lightly and as a consumer reporter I often hear from consumers who regret having done it. It will affect your credit history for seven full years and be permanently kept on file in Ottawa in a national database.

If you decide to move ahead with the bankruptcy process, your assets will be turned over to the trustee, who will notify all creditors of your bankruptcy and ensure that they no longer seek payment outside of the bankruptcy process. You will be required to attend financial counselling and you will be in bankruptcy for about nine months. During that time you will have to submit monthly statements of your income and expenses.

Declaring bankruptcy will eliminate most of your debts and provide immediate relief from legal actions by creditors. You sign over most of your personal property to a licensed trustee in bankruptcy. You will lose any equity in your home and car, as well as in RRSPs that are held by banks, brokerages or in self-directed funds. You do not have to turn over RRSPs associated with life insurance plans or money held in a company pension plan. (Proposed legislation in Ottawa, Bill C-55, would allow consumers to keep all forms of RRSPs and allow students to write off their student loans if they have been out of college or university seven years instead of the current 10. This legislation has not passed yet, however, and may not.)

Once a bankruptcy is under way, the trustee will sell your assets and use the money to pay off as much debt as possible. Any remaining debt, with certain exceptions such as court fines, alimonies or child support, is then legally eliminated. You will be allowed to retain certain things such as clothing, furniture and tools if they are required for your occupation. Laws regarding what you can and can't keep vary from province to province. To qualify for bankruptcy you must owe at least $1,000 and be unable to make regular payments on time, or owe more than the resale value of what you own.

If your affairs aren't complicated and you owe less than $75,000 excluding the mortgage on your residence, you can make a "division two proposal" or "consumer proposal" to creditors. It will help you avoid bankruptcy. Such a proposal may seek an extension of time for payment, reductions in interest rates and repayment of less than 100 cents on the dollar. If those who are owed money agree to a proposal, bankruptcy can be avoided.

Owing in excess of $75,000 is known as a "division one proposal," but in the event it is refused it leads to automatic bankruptcy. Many people facing bankruptcy are concerned about their long-term credit rating. However, if their debts are totally unmanageable, their credit rating may already be in an awful state; declaring bankruptcy might not be any worse.

Life After Bankruptcy

The bankruptcy information will come off your credit rating after seven years, unless you have been bankrupt more than once.

Once you have declared bankruptcy you will face extra scrutiny when you apply for credit in the future. You could have difficulty acquiring a credit card and may need to apply for a secured card, which is secured by funds you have deposited with a bank or credit union. You will have to tell potential lenders you have declared bankruptcy (they will know anyway), so you will have to try to convince them you're a good risk because of your current financial situation and employment income and not a bad risk because of your past mistakes. You may not be able to get loans or you could be penalized by paying higher interest rate charges.

Just to add insult to financial injury, you will have to pay about $1,500 to declare personal bankruptcy! Since you likely can't afford it, the trustee is paid with assets from the bankrupt estate. While the bankruptcy information does roll off your credit rating in seven years, it is permanently listed in Ottawa, something that's been done since 1978. For a fee of about $8, anyone can search the archives to see who has declared bankruptcy (see Industry Canada's website at www.ic.gc.ca for further details). If you find that you are having problems paying bills, you should speak to a credit counsellor before it gets to the point where bankruptcy becomes your only option. It's something you really don't want to do and with the proper financial planning it can be avoided.

avoiding credit repair agencies

If you are someone who has dug themselves into a deep hole and now has credit problems, don't expect a "credit repair agency" to come to the rescue. They won't and they can't. You may come across ads on the Internet, newspaper or radio that promise to clean up and erase your bad credit history. These companies call themselves credit advisors, credit rating correction services or credit consultants. The ads usually say something like "Can't get a loan because of bad credit? We can help!"

The truth is that no one can repair your credit file and erase your overspending ways. If you defaulted on loans and didn't make credit card payments on time, you can't just pay someone to remove your past mistakes. There is a legal time limit that your credit history must remain on file and there are no loopholes that any credit agency can use to have your credit history altered before that time is up. (Only the credit bureau can remove negative information, and that's only if it's incorrect; they'll correct the error for free.)

The federal government is concerned about a new trend in which credit repair companies not only promise to clean up your poor credit record, but also help you establish an entirely new credit identity. It's illegal to lie on credit applications, pretend to be someone else or use a different social insurance number. You should be cautious of any company that encourages you to omit or misrepresent your bad credit experience when you apply for new credit, or tells you to use a different name, address, phone number or social insurance number. Anyone who says it's all right to establish a new credit identity is telling you to break the law.

Another tactic used by credit repair agencies is to guarantee they can get you a car loan or credit card regardless of your credit history. Don't expect these companies to honour their guarantees. If you're dealing with them in the first place, chances are you are not in the best financial shape to go after them if they take your money and run. If you do get a credit card with their help, it may be a "secured" bank credit card with expensive up-front fees that require you to deposit money in a savings account as security. You could then be charged interest on your own money.

> Beware of credit repair companies that ask you to dial a "900" telephone number. It could cost you $2 or $3 a minute to find out useless information.

The best way to improve your credit rating is to use good credit practices. Eventually your past mistakes and bad credit history will roll off. Telling a lender up front about your credit problems before they find out about them (which they will) can improve your chances of getting a loan if you are able to show you have made a recent effort to improve your handling of credit.

PART 2

SAVING MONEY

Saving money is easy to talk about but hard to do. Temptation lurks around every corner ... a faster computer, a nicer car, a night on the town or a weekend away. All of it is something we want and of course the only way to get it is to spend money.

Learning how to say no to yourself takes discipline and if you're not used to doing it, changing your lifestyle will come as quite a shock. But it can be done and you will be surprised at how quickly your savings add up.

During the early days of my career as a general assignment reporter, I interviewed the latest lottery winners. When you see someone win $22 million, you realize why people might prefer to think about hitting the jackpot than worry about retirement. Well, consider these odds: The chance you'll win the jackpot in LOTTO SUPER 7 are 1 in 62,891,499. The odds for LOTTO 649 are better, at about 1 in 13,983,816. Many people are hoping they will strike it rich at the casino; gambling has become a huge and expensive pastime for Canadians. It seems everyone wants to get rich the easy way, but consider this calculation.

What if someone who spent $20 a week on lottery tickets or gambling saved it instead and was lucky enough to have a 10% return on their investment?

$20 a week x 52 weeks a year x 10% x 30 years = $206,329

$20 a week x 52 weeks a year x 10% x 40 years = $553,396

$20 a week x 52 weeks a year x 10% x 50 years = $1,453,598

Twenty bucks a week over 50 years equals almost one-and-a-half million dollars! Imagine saving your own jackpot! (I know, 50 years is a long time, but, hey, we're all living longer.) The point of this example is to show that even a small amount, just $20 a week, can become a fortune over time.

There is nothing wrong with buying lottery tickets and if you do, I hope you hit the jackpot, but don't count on winning the lottery or inheriting a fortune and ignore the need for a long-term financial plan. In the pages ahead we will look at ways to save on credit cards, car insurance and groceries. Whenever you spend money you will want to think how it will help you achieve your goals.

understanding interest rates

Of the main expenditures in our lives, there are only so many things we can control. A huge chunk of our paycheque goes to income, property and sales taxes. Then insurance costs gobble up more of our money as we pay premiums for home, car and life insurance.

There is one area, though, that is a huge expense in our lives, one that we can control, and that is how much money we spend on interest. Think of the tens of thousands of dollars we give banks for our homes, cars, personal loans, lines of credit and credit cards. In our lifetime we will spend hundreds of thousands of dollar on interest. It is interest charges that separate the consumers who get ahead from the ones who fall behind.

Trying to curtail the amount of interest we pay by trimming interest costs on our mortgage, avoiding high interest costs on car ownership and paying off credit cards is an essential part of a smart financial plan. Figure out just how much money you pay in interest charges every month and the amount may surprise you.

It's very possible that your monthly interest charges look like this:

Mortgage	$753
Car loan	$62
Consolidation loan	$54
Line of credit	$85
Credit cards	$68
Interest per month	$1,022

When you see just how much of your income is going to servicing debt, you will realize how important it is to pay down your debt to get ahead. While paying some interest may be necessary to function in our society, you can and should do everything possible to limit the amount of interest you pay. If it is not possible to pay "cash on the barrel," then you must take steps to make sure you are getting the lowest lending rate possible.

Keep an eye on interest rates, because interest is a positive and a negative factor on your finances. Compound interest will help your investments grow over time. But high interest rates on loans and debts have the opposite effect, causing you to fall behind as payments go toward interest charges rather than paying off the principal.

Interest rates on debt will fluctuate due to global market forces, the supply and demand for money, the current and expected rates of inflation, the length of time the funds are lent or borrowed and monetary policy. While Canada has been enjoying interest rates at historic lows, at some point they will go up. Depending on how much debt you have, a sharp increase in interest rates could have a dramatic and even devastating effect on your finances. Canada's central bank, the Bank of Canada, sets the bank rate and it is this rate that sets the standard for interest rates at all of Canada's major banks and financial institutions.

There are many variables that will affect how much the interest rate will be when you go to borrow money: whether the loan is secured or unsecured (a bank can repossess a car, but not a holiday in Mexico), your credit rating, the prevailing interest rates and your history with the bank or lender.

The business of lending money has become very competitive, so always keep in mind the posted rate at a bank is just a benchmark that you can use to *start* your negotiations. You should do the calculations for mortgages and car loans yourself before going to a lender so that you already know what the payments and interest will be. Loan calculators can be found by typing *loan calculator* into any search engine on the Internet or by visiting your own bank's website.

Go to a bank already aware of how much you want to borrow, the loan term in months and the interest rate you are prepared to pay. Check out the lending rates at other banks before agreeing to a loan and be a *shrewd negotiator!* Be ready to play hardball to try to get the lowest rate you can. You'll see that even negotiating an interest rate just half a percent lower can save you hundreds and even thousands of dollars over the long term. For example:

Home Loan

Mortgage amount	$250,000
Interest rate	7.5%
Amortization length	25 years
Monthly payment	$1,829
Total interest paid	$298,466

The same loan with an interest rate 0.50% lower looks like this:

Home Loan

Mortgage amount	$250,000
Interest rate	7%
Amortization length	25 years
Monthly payment	$1,751
Total interest paid	$275,147

You can see that by negotiating an interest rate just 0.50% lower, you can save $78 every month on this mortgage and over time you will pay the bank $23,319 less in interest costs! Imagine that—by simply negotiating half a percent in a banker's office, you can save more than $23,000. It's why it's so crucial to shop around for loans, especially a mortgage.

Making banks compete against each other for your business and letting them know you are looking for the best rate can help you get an interest rate break. After all, a bank would rather give you a loan at a slightly lower interest rate than lose your business altogether, and wouldn't you rather have the $23,000 in your account than theirs?

choosing the right credit card

While some consumer advocates want you to get out the scissors and cut up every credit card in your wallet, the truth is that for most of us, a credit card has become a necessity. Of course, if you have 12 of them you should start snipping (and of course contact the card companies to officially close the accounts!).

The Financial Consumer Agency of Canada says 40% of Canadians don't know the interest rate they are paying on their credit cards. *40%!* That's amazing but true; I once stopped shoppers outside a mall and asked them if they knew what interest rate they were paying on their credit cards and about half of them didn't know.

Too many consumers worry about point plans, air miles and other offers from credit card companies to think about their credit cards objectively. I interviewed one woman shopping in a department store who excitedly explained that if she spent another $500 she would be able to get a free coffee-maker. She would have been a lot better off simply buying the coffee-maker instead of going on a mad spending spree.

One of the best marketing campaigns I have seen in a long time is the credit card that has teamed up with a gas station to save you "two cents a litre" every time you use it. This is an excellent credit card loyalty program for the gas station, the credit card company and the consumer *if* they pay off their balance each month. Suppose you fill up your car once a week with 50 litres of gas, so you will pay 93 cents a litre at the pump instead of paying 95 cents. When you do the math, you find that the average person will save about a dollar each fill-up. If they buy gas once a week, they will save $52 a year. That's great if they're paying off their credit card balance every month, but if they're not, they're letting hundreds or even thousands of dollars pile up on a credit card that has an interest rate of 19%. That $52 of annual savings will quickly be gobbled up in interest charges. The same is true of credit cards that reward you with air miles. If you pay off your balance every month then you may eventually "earn" a free trip. If you don't, that free trip may really cost you plenty in interest charges.

If you carry a balance, which about half of all Canadians do, it's the interest rate, not the perks, that should determine the card best for you. Balance carriers should consider a value credit card that has an interest rate as low as 10%. Compare that to the 19% most credit cards charge in interest fees or the 28% some department stores charge.

Credit Card	Balance on Card	Interest Rate	Annual Interest Charges
Low-rate card	$2,500	10%	$250
Major credit card	$2,500	19%	$475
Department store card	$2,500	28%	$700

As you can see, department store cards are not worth having if you carry a balance. Getting a free blender for using your card is no bargain if you have paid the store $700 in interest. These cards make it almost impossible to pay off the balance.

If you have high-interest debt you should work to pay it off immediately, transfer it to a lower-interest-rate card or consider a consolidation loan at a much lower rate (and remember, you must close down that card's account). A low-rate value card may have an annual fee of $40 or so, but the cost is worth it if you are carrying debt on a credit card. Check with your bank; chances are they have one. Tell them you don't care about toasters or air miles, just the card with the lowest interest rate. It will save you money as you pay down your balance because more of your payment will go to the principal and not interest payments. This one low-interest credit card is all you need. Ensure you review your credit cards annually to see if they are still the best choice for you.

getting the best car insurance

Car insurance premiums have gone through the roof over the years. Rates depend on your age, marital status, gender, type of vehicle and your driving record. You should review your insurance costs often, since as long as you're driving you have insurance bills to pay, and the truth is that many people are paying too much. Auto insurance is under provincial jurisdiction. In British Columbia, Saskatchewan and Manitoba the government provides coverage, while in other provinces it's handled by private insurers. In Quebec, auto insurance is a public/private split, with physical damage and liability coverage provided by private insurers and bodily injury coverage provided by the government. While some provinces have "no-fault" insurance, this doesn't mean that drivers won't be penalized if they caused the crash. "No-fault" means that after an accident, claims are paid out quickly to avoid delays, but the insurance companies will still investigate to determine who's to blame and their insurance will go up.

Lee Romanov is the president of The Consumer's Guide to Insurance and runs the Internet-based insurance service www.insurancehotline.com. This website allows you to enter your personal information to find the insurance company with the best rates for you. It's been operating since 1994 and handles between two to three thousand quotes a day on car, motorcycle, home, life and business insurance. Romanov says, "Over the last 10 years the car insurance companies have really focused in on what they are looking at insuring. That means the spread between insurance rates has actually widened. It's really important now to match your profile with an insurance company that caters to what you drive, where you live and your driving record." Many people want to stay with their insurance company out of loyalty, thinking this will lead to lower rates, but that's not necessarily true. I take many calls from irate drivers who say they've been with a company for 20 years but won't be renewed because of two speeding tickets. Romanov explains, "Whether you've been with an insurance company 20 minutes or 20 years they have filed regulations with the government on the kind of business they will accept and the kind of business they won't accept on renewal. If you don't match what they will accept, they will non-renew you."

Minimizing Your Car Insurance Costs

To keep your insurance costs as low as possible you need to:

- keep a clean driving record
- always keep your insurance active
- renew your licence on time
- take part in group insurance
- choose the best insurance company for you
- make yourself a desired insurance risk
- make only necessary claims
- take only necessary coverage
- fight every ticket
- avoid being labeled "at fault" in an accident
- consider how new drivers affect your policy rates

Keep a Clean Driving Record

At-fault accidents and driving convictions such as speeding tickets and other traffic violations will cause your rates to increase dramatically. Serious offences such as dangerous driving or impaired driving will cause long-term harm and expense. According to Romanov, "There are cases where if you have had three minor tickets they will non-renew you. In some cases if you have had two minor tickets and one accident they will non-renew you. Every insurance company has its own regulations, the same way they have their own rates for every particular car and driver."

Keep Your Insurance Active

I get complaints from viewers who have mistakenly let their insurance run out. They may have been on a holiday or they may have sold one car and were waiting a month or two before buying another. You should never let your insurance lapse! Doing this can dramatically affect your rates and cause you to start over as a new driver with some insurance companies. Romanov agrees this is how rates can skyrocket. "You never want to let your insurance lapse. You may find yourself being thrown into a nonstandard, high-risk market known as the facility market, and there are only about six or seven markets out there that will take high-risk drivers and their rates are extremely high." If you drive a company car and decide to give up your own personal car and insurance, you should ask your insurance company if this will affect your rates. (If your company keeps a record of your personal driving experience there shouldn't be a problem. If they have blanket or fleet coverage and can't identify which individuals had accidents, it could pose a problem.)

Renew Your Licence on Time

You'll also run into trouble if you don't renew your driver's licence on time. Some drivers get their slip in the mail but don't renew it until three or four months later. That shows up on your driver's abstract and can create the same kind of problem with an insurance company as tickets and accidents. Romanov warns, "It could be enough to put you into a high-risk market or cause you to have to retake your driver's licence." If you're late renewing and it shows up on your motor vehicle driver's abstract, your insurance company may see that you have been driving without a licence and jack up your rates substantially.

Take Part in Group Insurance

One thing that I would definitely recommend is group insurance. We have a plan where I work and it has brought my insurance premiums down hundreds of dollars. The idea is that while most insurance companies have to draw on the general population, companies or professional groups such as nurses or teachers have already been pre-screened so they must adhere to a certain level of conduct to be employed in that profession. Romanov says, "There are companies that cater to groups and you should look into it and see what your quote is. I don't think that should stop you from checking out other insurance companies as well, because sometimes the group rates don't cater to what you particularly drive or your driving history."

Choose the Best Insurance Company for You

The single best thing you can do, according to Romanov, is make sure you are matched with the best insurance company for your profile. The most obvious way you can do this is finding a company with the lowest rates for your driving situation. For example, when an insurance company jacks up someone's rates from $1,500 a year to $5,000 annually these are "go away rates"; the company is basically telling you to go away! It's the first clue you should start looking around for another company to insure you.

Make Yourself a Desired Insurance Risk

Where you live, how far you commute, multi-vehicle discounts, and the make and model of your vehicle will also have a big impact on premiums. Some cars cost more to repair, have fewer safety features or may be targeted by thieves. The Canadian Loss Experience Automobile Rating (CLEAR) system rewards car owners with lower premiums for buying vehicles that experience fewer and smaller losses. For information on car ratings, contact the Vehicle Information Centre of Canada (VICC) at www.vicc.com.

Make Only Necessary Claims

You also definitely don't want to be making claims. Unfortunately, many drivers are now self-insuring or subsidizing insurance companies by repairing their own scratches, dents and windshield cracks. As maddening as it can be to pay to repair your own car when you're paying for insurance, it really is wise to look after minor repairs. "Insurance companies base their rates on risk whether you paid for the claim, whether they paid for the claim and whether the claim was $70,000 or $300. A claim is a claim," says Romanov. "Insurance really isn't meant for maintenance. It's really directed toward catastrophic loss. You really want to save the big stuff for the insurance companies."

Take Only Necessary Coverage

You can save money by raising your deductible or taking collision off an older vehicle. Once your car reaches 200,000 kilometres or is eight to 10 years old, depending on the model it may only be worth $2,000 or $3,000. You could save $300 to $500 a year by declining collision insurance (the coverage that pays for repairs if you're in a crash). If the car is worth several thousand dollars there is some risk in case you do get into a fender-bender; however, even then you will have to pay the $500 deductible to get the car repaired. Don't take collision off a car too soon, but don't waste money insuring an old clunker, either.

Fight Every Ticket

You should also be aware that when you get a ticket from a police officer, whether it's for speeding, not wearing a seatbelt or because you forgot your licence at home, it could affect your insurance. Romanov is adamant that you should fight every ticket in court just in case you get another one shortly after. She insists, "You may not think that one ticket matters, but if you have one ticket and then six months later you get into an accident and if it's your fault, you could get a second ticket as well. With some insurance companies, two tickets and one accident can cause you to be non-renewed even if you've had 25 years with a perfect driving record. It could happen fast and your rates could increase by thousands of dollars overnight." Even U.S. and out-of-province tickets can show up on your driving record. Most provinces and states have reciprocity agreements, so your speeding ticket in Florida or New York could affect your insurance when you get home. It's not a perfect system; sometimes the tickets show up and sometimes they don't. And fighting a ticket doesn't mean pleading guilty with an explanation. "Never plead guilty with an explanation, because it's just saying you're guilty. They may lower the fine, but a ticket is a ticket. What you need to do is plead not guilty and leave it up to the courts to prove that you are guilty."

If you get one speeding ticket, half of the insurance companies in Canada will raise your rates and half won't, so one ticket could cause your insurance rates to go up anywhere from zero to $500. Two tickets can mean increases of $500 to $1,500 and an accident can increase rates anywhere from $1,000 to $2,000; some companies actually have a spread of up to $8,000 if you have an accident. Tickets stay on your record for three years and accidents for six years.

It's good to know that red light camera or photo radar tickets do not appear on your driver's abstract. The reason is that they can't identify the driver; they can only identify the car. So if you were going to fight a ticket you should be more inclined to fight one given to you by an officer than you would a machine. Keep in mind as well that when an officer says they will reduce a fine so you won't get demerit points, a ticket is a ticket, whether you get points taken off or not. It could take you five tickets to affect your licence but just one or two could greatly affect your insurance rates. If your premiums do go from $2,000 a year to $7,000, the insurance company is basically telling you to go elsewhere and you should (but they'll accept your money if you choose to stay with them).

Avoid Being Labeled "At Fault"

Romanov points out it's important to try to make sure you are never labeled at fault in an accident. Even when following through with the adjuster you have to ensure that you are not even labeled partially at fault. "If they classify you as partially at fault, you might as well be completely at fault rate-wise with an insurance company." In a lot of situations people talk themselves into tickets and careless driving charges even though they weren't being careless. An example would be if you get into an accident and then you say to the police officer, 'I didn't see the car' as opposed to 'I didn't see the car until it was too late.'" The first situation is careless driving. The second one is not.

Consider How New Drivers Affect Your Policy Rates

Get ready to open your wallet wide if you have a teenager who will be driving the family car. As soon as your child gets their G1 or G2 the game changes. Their rates are so high that what you now need to do is find the insurance company with the lowest rates for the youngest driver and the youngest male driver in your family. Romanov says, "The kids now direct which insurance company you should be with because the spread of rates are greatest for them." New drivers should take a driver's training course, which could help them reduce rates by as much as 30%.

Remember, while your insurance is valid in Canada and the United States, you need additional insurance once you enter Mexico. For more information on insurance, check the Insurance Bureau of Canada's website at www.ibc.ca. You can also compare insurance rates at Romanov's www.insurancehotline.com, where 80% of insurance companies are represented. The site will give you the top three companies with the best rates for your situation and contact information. The quotes are free, but in some circumstance there may be a charge of about $10 if a person has multiple tickets and accidents and it is difficult to find a company to insure them. It really is worth checking out.

Obtaining Gap Insurance

Gap insurance is for customers who lease cars or take a loan to buy them, although most insurance companies offer it only on new cars, not used ones. For only a few dollars a month, gap insurance will pay the difference between what you owe and what the vehicle is worth in the event the car is stolen or written off in an accident. A brand new car will nosedive in value as soon as you drive it off the lot. So what happens if the car is stolen, in a fire or a serious accident?

If you have contracted with a leasing company to make payments of $450 a month for 48 months, this means you've agreed to pay a total of $21,600. If, 10 months in, you have a serious accident and the car is written off by your insurance company, they may assess the car's value at $15,000. You have only made 10 payments so according to the contract you still owe the leasing company $17,100. The insurance company only has to pay you the fair market value of the car, so you are on the hook for the difference of $2,100. Many people assume an insurance payout will always be enough to tidy up loose ends and pay off the remaining lease payments, but that's not always the case. Gap insurance would pay that $2,100.

The same is true of a vehicle loan. Suppose you borrowed $40,000 over five years at 7% interest. Your monthly payment is $792. Your total obligation with interest is $47,523. If you experience total loss you could owe the bank more than the vehicle's fair market value, which is all your insurance payout will be. Gap insurance will protect you.

When leasing or buying a new car, ask your insurance agent to include gap insurance. It would be unfortunate in the event of a total loss of a vehicle to have to pay thousands of dollars to clean up a lease or loan for a car you can no longer drive.

buying life and disability insurance

No one likes to talk about the unexpected, unfortunate events in our lives, but not planning for death or potential disability won't make them any less difficult for you and your family if and when they strike.

Life Insurance

We've all heard people remark, "I'm worth more dead than alive." Unfortunately, this may be true, because many of us want to make sure there is enough money left behind to keep loved ones comfortable and financially secure in the event of our untimely death.

It's not pleasant to think about, but what if you died tomorrow? What if your spouse died? Would your family be able to stay in their current home? Would your children be able to attend college or university? Could your family afford daycare, vacations and the lifestyle they've become accustomed to?

Some form of life insurance coverage is crucial to almost any financial plan. If you're single with no dependants, you may feel you don't need life insurance, or you could have coverage and make the beneficiary a brother, sister, parent, niece or charity. You should make sure you have at least enough insurance to cover your funeral costs so that the expense and undue hardship on a retired parent or family member with limited income can be avoided. Once you have a life insurance policy, you can change jobs, remarry or become seriously ill, and no matter what happens you will be covered.

You will have to decide how much coverage you need and what kind to choose. Some financial planners say that five to seven times your current income is enough. Three times is the minimum you should have as long as you have mortgage insurance to ensure your home will be paid off if you were to die.

While polices may have different names or descriptions, generally speaking, there are three kinds of insurance to choose from: term, term to 100 and permanent.

Term. This is the most inexpensive type of life insurance policy because it's basically pay as you go. It's chunks of insurance in five-, 10- or 20-year terms. The younger you are, the cheaper the premiums. The premiums increase as you get older and renewability of coverage will terminate, usually at age 65. The policy also has no cash surrender value, so if you close down the policy while you're alive you won't get any money back. (Still, that's a good thing!)

Term to 100. A term-to-100 plan is basically unending, no frills term insurance. This kind of plan can provide you protection until you are 100 years old if kept in force. The premium cost is lower than permanent polices, but again, there is no cash surrender value.

Permanent. Permanent life insurance is also known as whole life or universal life insurance. It provides an investment component as well as a cash value option. If you agree to give up the death benefit, you can cash in the policy for money that has built up in the plan. Whole and universal plans cover you for your entire life and your premiums won't change. Your payments will be determined based on your age, job, health and other risk factors. One of the major drawbacks to this type of coverage is that it can be very expensive; you will have to pay huge premiums every month. If you terminate early, your insurance will be canceled and there will be penalties to pay. Even though the premiums are expensive, it could take as long as 10 years before the cash values in the plan become sizable enough to offer you adequate insurance protection.

You can buy life insurance several ways. The most common is through an insurance broker. Your company may offer some form of life insurance through a payroll deduction plan, and you also have the option of taking out life insurance on your mortgage through your bank.

Always be honest on your life insurance forms! If you have a history of heart disease or still smoke behind your spouse's back it could cause the policy to be voided in the future. Once you disclose any health problems and your life insurance policy is in place (and you're making payments), then you're covered. I do get complaints from viewers who are diagnosed with a serious medical condition and have difficulty trying to get life insurance or insurance becomes unaffordable. Still, be wary of life insurance policies advertisements that promise low monthly premiums with no medical exam. (You know the ones. It's Gloria on the phone, and she's just bought life insurance!) The payments may be low but the payout will be too. I've heard from families who have paid $10,000 in premiums on these limited polices only to get back $6,000 when the individual died.

Coverage can be complex, so be careful not to get talked into any life insurance plan without knowing exactly what you are signing up for. You should also be aware that most life insurance agents are paid a commission by the insurance company issuing the product. For many people, term insurance may be the best choice because it is a way to have coverage as you pay down your mortgage or raise your children. You don't want to pay too much for insurance, but you want to make sure you have adequate coverage to protect your family.

For free information on all life insurance matters, you can go to the Canadian Life and Health Insurance Association's Consumer Assistance Centre. It is a non-profit, non-sales line in French and English that has been in operation since 1973. For answers to any life insurance questions, call 1-800-268-8099 or check out the website, www.clhia.ca.

Disability Insurance

Disability insurance is essentially income replacement insurance that you buy in case an accident leaves you alive but unable to work. While many of us believe becoming disabled won't happen to us, statistics show that half of all mortgage foreclosures are due to disability. One of our most important assets is our ability to earn income. Once this is taken away from of us, it can have devastating consequences in our lives because your bills don't stop when your income stops.

Lifetime Earnings

If a worker is 35 years old and earns $5,000 a month in gross income, and his salary increased 5% a year, by the time he was 65 years old he would earn $3,986,331 in income. This just goes to show how productive a person is and the amount of income they could lose if they became permanently disabled.

While most people recognize the need for life insurance, many do not realize just how important disability insurance is. According to the insurance industry, if a disability lasts at least 90 days it is likely to last three years or more for a 35-year-old person or four years or more for a 45-year-old person. This is why you must take into consideration what would happen to your financial situation if you had a serious accident or illness.

You can get disability coverage from individual insurance plans (about 750,000 Canadians have their own individual policies), government plans (Worker's Compensation or Employment Insurance) or group insurance plans (through your employer, union or professional association). Usually you will also have disability coverage through auto insurance polices in case you become disabled in a car accident. These plans will pay between 65% and 80% of your gross earnings and the payouts may or may not be tax free. (If they paid more than that, you might not want to return to work.) There are three types.

Non-cancelable. The policy can't be canceled during the contract and the price cannot be raised.

Guaranteed renewable. The insurer must renew the policy but can raise premiums.

Commercial. On the anniversary, the insurer can decline to renew the policy or charge more to reflect previous claims.

Here's what happens if you become sick or injured. Group plans through employers cover you for short-term sick leave, up to two weeks of illness. When your sick days run out, you will then go on short-term disability. This will pay about 70% of your earnings for 15, 26 or 52 weeks. After this, you will go on long-term disability, which will last two years if you can't do your normal job and longer if you can't do any job.

If you are self–employed, you really should have some kind of disability insurance to save your business in the event you or your partner becomes ill or disabled. How much disability insurance you need depends on your lifestyle, family responsibilities, debts, financial resources and long-term dreams and goals.

If you have questions regarding disability insurance, you can call the information centre of The Canadian Life and Health Insurance Association at 1-800-268-8099 or check out its website, www.clhia.ca.

Life and disability insurance don't have to be expensive. They both can give you peace of mind as you pay down debt and save money, working your way toward wealth.

doing your income taxes

We all feel we pay too much tax. We pay tax on our paycheques, our property, gasoline and almost everything we buy. When you think about how much tax we pay, it's amazing how many people don't bother to try to fully understand their own tax situation.

I always look in bewilderment at people in their 40s, 50s and 60s sitting outside a tax preparation kiosk in a mall because they have no idea how to do their taxes. I know people who say they don't understand how the tax system works so they give a shoebox full of receipts to their accountant and let them figure it out. Only about half of us complete our own tax returns. If you have a complicated tax situation, such as a business or an income property, you may really require the involvement of a tax professional, but some people let someone else do it just because they have no desire to figure out how to fill out a tax return. Take the time to understand your tax situation—it's an area where you can save hundreds to thousands of dollars a year.

Evelyn Jacks is the author of 30 books on personal finance, and her 2005 book, *Essential Tax Facts*, has 235 tax tips that people should be aware of. Jacks says, "Knowing even a little bit about your taxes can bring huge, huge benefits. Your knowledge is going to be cumulative. You can't know it all at once but people should jump in because I am willing to bet that everyone who tries will find immediate benefits that can be turned around as new capital to help get them out of debt." With the tax software that's available, doing your taxes is now easier than ever. The tax programs can walk you through and help you find out not only if you are filling out your return properly, but they can also give you ideas about how to pay less tax next year. "I strongly believe every Canadian should do their own tax return at least once in their life and they should take it upon themselves to teach their children to do their own tax returns as well. Gone are the days of complicated repetitive calculations involving federal and provincial tax tables. Now the software does it for you," says Jacks.

Even if you have a fairly general return, it can be worth it to see a professional to ask questions and to ensure you are filling out your return correctly and getting every deduction you deserve. Jacks says, "The data that you are entering into your return is very important because a tax return can be done correctly many different ways. Your objective is to do your return to your family's absolute benefit and that's where many Canadians miss out." The tax department won't know if you had a baby, started a small business or sent a teenager off to university unless you tell them, so if information is not entered correctly you can miss out on thousands of dollars in credits and deductions. If a senior has been confined to a wheelchair and did not know they are entitled to the disability amount, that could cost them just under $2,000 a year. Jacks says, "My motto has always been there is no such thing as a stupid tax question. You know what's going on in your life and your tax advisor needs to know because it all comes down to the amount of money that can end up in your pocket." Finding out how to maximize your tax savings can help you get a larger refund, which can be applied against your debt. Many people need to change their approach.

I am always surprised when someone files their taxes late and incurs late filing charges. Why would someone do this? Your taxes affect you all year long and with every paycheque so filing is not a surprise, and most Canadians should look forward to tax time because they'll receive a refund, which is really a payback of your interest-free loan to the government.

Part of a solid financial plan is understanding how taxes affect your income. If you haven't been doing your own taxes, buy a tax software program and do them. If you have done your own taxes for many years, it's worth it to go to an accountant to ensure you are doing them correctly. There may be a cost of $100 to $150, but it will be well worth it if they find one area where you can save money. It can also give you peace of mind that you are doing your taxes correctly. You should dig and dig for every deduction that you're entitled to. If you don't fight for your tax money, no one else will!

hitting the sweet spot

I was with someone when the iPod music player first came out years ago. "Can we make a quick stop?" he asked. "Sure, what for?" I wondered. He wanted to be the first one to get the new iPod. The price tag was about $1,000. This person already had a music player but needed to have the newest and the best. I looked in disbelief as he plunked down his credit card to pay a thousand dollars for this little music device.

Now, we all know that the iPod has become one of the most popular music devices of our time, but within a few short years the price of the iPod dropped first 20%, then 40% and now almost 70%. They are not only cheaper, they're better, too. The iPods sold now hold more music, are easier to use and are more dependable. There are even mini iPods for about $100.

This is not a fluke. As sure as taxes will rise, consumer goods will drop in price because they are mass-produced. The first people who must have the iPod, plasma TV or digital video recorder are helping pay for the research and development costs. All of these consumer goods improve over time as flaws and kinks are worked out. (Many people contacted me to complain about the first plasma TVs that suffered permanent "burn in" on the screen because of

TV station graphics that were constantly on screen—like a station logo in the corner.) It's one of the ironies that the people who are the last to buy digital cameras, camcorders and laptops end up with better products at a cheaper price than those who had to have them right away.

This is the "sweet spot"—that place where a consumer good has become popular enough to be mass-produced, the price has fallen and the design flaws and kinks have been worked out. When buying any consumer product, this is the zone you want the item to be in. Hitting the sweet spot may be easier to do with some products than others, but it can always be done. And until the sweet spot happens, the product likely isn't worth getting. Who needs a product with a format that doesn't match with others, that wasn't popular enough to have extra parts produced or can't be repaired because it has been discontinued? Whether it was the CD player, DVD player, digital camera or HDTV, they all started out very expensive and dropped in price.

Never be in a hurry to buy into new technology. Let the Joneses buy it first. You can always get it later when it's better and cheaper.

trimming the grocery bill

Benjamin Franklin said, "A fat kitchen makes a lean will," and he was right. I was behind someone at the grocery store who was shopping with her son. They had two grocery carts jammed full of all kinds of prepared food, junk food, comfort food and a few of the necessary staples. While I'm usually not that interested in what people are buying, I was shocked when their food bill rang in at more than $450! It didn't look like they were preparing for a party, either. This seemed to be what they were buying on a regular basis.

Many people now spend more money every month on food than they do on their car! That makes buying groceries the second-highest monthly expense after paying your mortgage or rent. Many people don't think to include food in their financial planning because it's a necessity and we need it to survive; however, this is one area where people lose control every week and overspend.

> Saving just $20 a week on your grocery bill can save you more than $1,000 a year. Saving $60 a week could help you save more than $3,000 a year.

I first met Kimberly Clancy when we did a story on *Canada AM* about trying to save money on your grocery bill. Clancy runs her own website, www.frugalshopper.ca. The site is a wealth of frugal knowledge, where Canadians can go to find out about sales from coast to coast, free shopping advice, coupon tips and ideas on how to shave money off their grocery bill. I went shopping with Clancy and the two of us had the exact same shopping list. The money she saved was amazing.

Without using coupons, I spent	$133.89
Using coupons, Clancy spent	$23.45
That's a savings of	$110.44

Imagine saving $110 on your grocery bill! On this visit Clancy did use some freebie coupons she was saving up for our demonstration, but she says she routinely saves about 25% or more on her grocery bill every week using coupons, flyers and watching for sales.

Clancy says, "I think many people spend way too much money on groceries, especially when you go to the premium grocery stores. These high-end chains will have beautiful layouts, fancy displays and better lighting, but most premium outlets also own a budget grocery chain that has prices that can be 30% cheaper and the food comes from the same warehouse."

One way to save on your grocery bill is to buy store or generic brands instead of national brands. They are usually much cheaper and just as good. (National brands have to hike their prices up to pay off those expensive TV commercials and magazine ads.) Beans that are canned for more expensive national brands are the same beans that go into the cans sold under the store's name brand. I'll never forget touring a bottled water facility and seeing water going into different bottles with different labels. It was the exact same water being bottled, but the prices ranged from $0.89 a bottle to $1.59 for the same H_2O! Often, no-name camera film, batteries and blank CDs are also manufactured by the same companies that produce the more expensive national brand. It just makes sense to try the cheaper brand, and if it works or tastes fine then stick with it.

One of the best ways to save money on your grocery list is to make sure you know the prices of the products you use often. "You won't know what a good deal is if you don't know what the prices are. Just because it's on sale doesn't mean it's a bargain. When you use coupons and other promotional offers you'll get even more savings," says Clancy. The best sale items will be on the front and back of the flyer and when there is something on sale you use regularly, stock up!

Warehouse shopping and buying in bulk are also good ideas, but you can easily walk into a warehouse store with the best intentions to save money and walk out with only eight items that cost you $150, so care must be taken here as well.

Grocery Shopping Do's
- Do plan ahead
- Do use meal plans
- Do get organized
- Do avoid impulse shopping

Grocery Shopping Don'ts
- Don't shop on credit
- Don't buy name brands
- Don't buy junk food
- Don't buy food you're not sure you'll eat
- Don't shop when you're hungry

Admittedly, I'm not someone who would spend much time clipping coupons and many of us would find it hard to make the effort or find the energy to bother. While manufacturers issue about 2.6 billion coupons a year, only 97 million coupons are redeemed. Many people who do clip coupons are stay-at-home parents, retirees and students, but Clancy says everyone can benefit. "Everyone has to eat and anyone who wants to save money can. Food is something we have to buy anyway and you should try to find savings, especially if you are spending hundreds of dollars a week on groceries." With all her coupon clipping, Clancy says she spends only about $50 a week to feed her family. "If you cut back a little you can save a little, and if you cut back a lot you can really save a lot. It's that simple."

renting
to own

Why would you rent to own anything? Other than in a few very specific situations, renting to own is a terrible financial move. Don't do it. Renting to own is a system set up by financial predators to bilk cash-strapped low-income earners out of their money. You need a new fridge and can't afford one? We'll rent you one. Want a new TV for the Super Bowl but don't have the cash? We'll rent you one and maybe one day it will be yours (sure, once you've paid two, three or four times what it's worth).

The best way to buy anything is with cash. Need a dishwasher but don't have the money? You may be tempted to put it on a credit card or payment plan, and either option is better than renting. Rent-to-own centres cater to consumers with no savings, a poor credit history or just an insatiable itch to get a stereo fast with no money down. You may be swayed by low weekly or monthly payments, free delivery, instant approvals and free repairs, but it doesn't matter. It's almost always a rotten deal. Consider this: If you rent a washer and dryer set for $24 a week for 112 weeks, the total rental price is $2,688. If the washer and dryer could have been purchased for $1,150, you have paid $1,538 more for the set than it was worth!

There are only a few instances where renting to own might be a viable option. If you're starting a small business and need equipment, renting can get you up and running until you can purchase equipment of your own. If you had to relocate for work or are a student going to school somewhere for a short period of time, renting could save you from having to move appliances or furniture across the country. If you are going through a divorce you may want to rent appliances until you receive your share of household articles under a divorce settlement. Still, for most people, a better route than renting to own is buying something used out of the classified ads or at a used appliance store.

A Note to People in Ontario

Do you still rent your hot water heater? Why? You likely don't rent your stove or computer, so why are you still renting your hot water heater? In most other regions of the country, consumers have figured out you should own your hot water heater instead of renting it. It's just a giant kettle, but the gas company has done an excellent job of convincing some consumers they should pay $12 to $16 a month to rent it. This is similar to when people used to rent phones from the phone company (some still do) instead of buying them.

If you're renting a hot water heater, phone your gas company and ask them how much it will cost to buy it. I have purchased two homes in my life and immediately bought the hot water heater as soon as I moved in. (Each was less than $100—and then I had no more rental fees!)

More and more people are now buying their hot water heaters (especially since I did a story on this on CTV), so the gas company is now charging a removal fee to try to recoup some of the cash they are losing from people figuring out this "cash cow." Even if you do have to pay a fee, it may make sense for you to buy a hot water heater either from the gas company or a home supplies store.

The key is don't rent it—own it! You will save hundreds and possibly thousands of dollars over the life of the hot water heater. It's also a good selling feature when you sell your home. You can tell the prospective buyer, "Oh, and don't worry about hot water heater rental fees. I own the hot water heater and I will throw it in as part of the deal." You wouldn't want to move it anyway.

---

keeping cash register scanners honest

Did you know that if a cash register rings up the wrong price on an item at the checkout, you may be entitled to get it for free or $10 off? Well, it's true.

The Scanner Price Accuracy Voluntary Code was introduced June 11, 2002, and is designed to keep store checkouts in Canada accurate and honest. It has been endorsed by Industry Canada's Competition Bureau and is designed to demonstrate retailer commitment to price scanner accuracy. More than 5,000 Canadian stores have agreed to honour it. While it's the law in Quebec and voluntary in the rest of Canada, most consumers still don't know about it, but you should. Here's what it says:

> On a claim being presented by the customer, where the scanned price of a product at a checkout is higher than the price displayed in the store or than advertised by the store, the lower price will be honoured; and (a) if the correct price of the product is $10 or less, the retailer will give the product to the customer free of charge; or (b) if the correct price of the product is higher than $10, the retailer will give the customer a discount of $10 off the corrected price.

So if the wrong price comes up on a can of tuna or jar of pickles, it's free. If you're buying a more expensive item like a drill at a hardware store, then you're entitled to $10 off. The biggest overcharges are usually found in department stores and home improvement centres, usually because goods are priced higher than grocery store items. Either way, it pays to pay attention. If you have a full cart and are tossing your groceries on the conveyor belt, a good checkout clerk can have them scanned and into bags before you know it. That's why you should be watching as your goods are being scanned in. The consumer also has to catch the mistake and be aware of the policy. Stores don't go to great lengths to let people know about it since every inaccurate price that's rung up will cost them money.

Some stores have installed self-scanning technology so that consumers can scan, bag and pay for groceries themselves. This means you can scan at your own speed, checking prices as you go along.

The Competition Bureau first rang the alarm on scanner accuracy in 1996 when it conducted a price accuracy survey of 162 businesses including grocery, drug and department stores. Out of 15,000 items purchased, there was a combined average error rate of 6.3%. This included a 3.0% overcharge rate and a 3.3% undercharge rate, so the mistakes were not always in favour of the store. Technophiles were quick to point out that the mistakes with the scanning technology, which reads the Universal Product Codes, known as UPC symbols or bar codes, were the fault of human error and not the technology itself. Most pricing errors are the result of a clerk failing to enter prices correctly, stockers not changing pricing on the shelf and stores not switching prices when items are on sale.

In 2005, a new 14-digit bar code was introduced worldwide, expanding on the current 12- and 13-digit bar codes used by retailers, and there are fears that as adjustments are made to stock and databases there may be even more mistakes at the checkout. So what can you do? Watch closely as purchases are rung in, especially sale items where most of the mistakes are made. You may wish to keep goods on sale at the beginning or the back of the conveyor belt so you can watch them as they are scanned in. Take flyers with you when you shop so you can point out to the clerk the true price in case of a mistake, and double-check your receipts at home. If you see a pattern of incorrect pricing, report it to the store manager.

Now that you know about the policy, you should use it. The next time an incorrect price pops up on the register when you're shopping, tell the clerk you're aware the Scanner Price Accuracy Voluntary Code and that you want your free can of soup or $10 off the lawn mower. I'm going to try it from now on. Ten bucks is ten bucks, and it's the only way to get stores to become more accurate.

If you have a scanning complaint that cannot be dealt with at the store level, call the Scanner Price Accuracy Committee at 1-866-499-4599. You can also go to the Retail Council of Canada's website at www.retailcouncil.org to find out more about the policy and see the list of stores that have agreed to abide by it.

refusing extended warranties

Buy anything these days and chances are you will be pitched an extended warranty along with it. "Don't you want to protect your investment?" It's amazing how a salesperson will spend 10 minutes telling you how great something is, only to then tell you how it's likely to break down and need repairs once you've bought it.

You should know that extended warranties, also called service agreements, are a profit generator for stores—a cash cow. That's why employees are pushed by upper management to sell them and are especially eager to do so if they are on commission.

Extended warranties can be expensive, at as much as 20% of the purchase price of the product. If you buy a $100 DVD player, you don't really need to spend another $20 just in case something goes wrong with it. It probably comes with a one-year warranty anyway, and if you buy it using a major credit card like a Visa or MasterCard, in most cases the warranty doubles so you are already up to two years' protection. Also, chances are, if something is going to go wrong with it, it usually happens not long after you get it home.

Consumer Reports magazine studied repair rates on consumer goods and found that extended warranties are rarely worth buying.

Statistics show that the odds a product will fail in the first five years are one in four. Depending on what you've purchased you may want to replace it rather than fix it anyway. The cost of a repair could also be close to what you would have paid for the extended warranty in the first place.

Extended warranties may be from a third party, so you may not even get service from the store you bought it from. Another tier of customer service can lead to delays.

If you do buy an extended warranty, never lose your paperwork, as the company may say the onus is on you to prove that you do have coverage. No paperwork could equal no coverage.

Extended warranties are sometimes worth having and there may be extra features that make them worth considering. When we bought our refrigerator, we were told that if we purchased an extended warranty for $100 we would receive three water filters (for the water dispenser and ice maker) that were worth $30 each, so it seemed like the warranty was worth getting. As luck would have it, the ice maker quit working two years later and did need service (I have since found out there is a big problem with ice makers in refrigerators). In this case, it paid off for us. Extended warranties may also be a good idea for expensive television sets, treadmills and laptop computers, because they can be expensive to fix.

I get many consumers asking me about extended warranties for cars. The general rule is that warranties offered through car manufacturers and new car dealers are more reliable than warranties offered by used car dealers (third parties). That doesn't mean that when your three-year warranty on your car is up you should pay another $1,500 to extend it. Many of these warranties are expensive and offer extremely limited protection. I've had complaints from the public about used car warranties that say they will only cover new parts that fail. Well, every part on a used car is used, so the warranty is useless.

Usually you are better off putting the money for the warranty in the bank. That way you will have the money there for your first repair, and if there are no breakdowns you will be ahead.

The best advice is not to get pressured into agreeing to spend more money on extended warranties just because a salesperson is advising you it's a good move. You should spend as much time considering the warranty as you did the item you were purchasing.

unearthing unclaimed balances

Is there a chance that you have unclaimed money in the bank? Most of us would say no, because money is scarce and it's not often we would allow any to go missing. But the truth is that 750,000 Canadians have left money behind in banks accounts. There is over $225 million in unclaimed money piled up in a vault in Ottawa just waiting for someone to claim it. Is some of it yours?

When I did a story on unclaimed bank balances for CTV's *Canada AM*, I heard from Canadians across the country who were excited to find out they were getting an unexpected payday. I found money for a 93-year-old man, a Toronto hospital, a minor hockey team and the Canadian Cancer Society. I heard from people like Bonnie, who wrote, "Thanks for the story on forgotten bank accounts. I had money in the Bank of Canada I forgot about! A nice sum too—$500! I'm going through the process of claiming it right now." Lawrence wrote, "Thanks for the tip on unclaimed balances. I was in the military and moved quite frequently. I'd forgotten about an old savings account from 21 years ago. There was just over $500 in it, which will come in handy."

How do we lose track of our money? People move around, get deposits they didn't know about or for whatever reason have just forgotten they have an account. Once money sits dormant in a Canadian bank account for 10 years without the bank being able to contact the owner, it must be sent off to Ottawa and the Bank of Canada for safekeeping. Balances of $500 or more will be kept indefinitely until they are claimed. If it's less than $500, you've got 20 years (10 at the bank branch and then another 10 at the Bank of Canada). After that it's too late, and the money becomes the property of the Canadian government.

Finding out if you have unclaimed money is just a couple of mouse clicks away. It's a free service and it's definitely something you should try. Go to the Bank of Canada website (www.bankof-canada.ca), select the *Services* menu and click on *Unclaimed Balances*. Follow the links, type in your name and hope for the best!

Also try names of family members, friends, local charities, churches and sports teams. If you do find unclaimed cash, it's not automatically yours—you do have to prove you are the legitimate owner. You will have to show that you had prior dealings with the bank that turned over the funds and explain why you left the money behind.

There are forms to fill out to prove you are the rightful owner of the forgotten cash and you will have to provide your signature for comparison purposes. The bank will also want to see an original bank passbook, bank statement or some kind of proof you resided at the address used for the bank account. It will take 30 to 60 days for you to receive your funds. If you're an heir to the estate of the owner of an unclaimed balance, or an officer of an organization or charity, you must contact the bank directly.

A full list of unclaimed balances may also be purchased on a CD-ROM for $72 plus GST and PST, plus $3 for shipping. Of course, if you have Internet access, just go online and give it a try. If you don't find money for you, you may for a family member, friend or charity in your area. There is nothing quite like an unexpected payday.

PART 3

PLANNING FOR WEALTH

Now that you know it is possible to pay down debt and save money, you will have to start planning what you will do once you start accumulating wealth. At this point in the book it should be clear that the problem most people have with money is overspending—buying things they don't need and can't afford. We know that consolidating debt without taking a hard look at our spending patterns dooms us to repeat the same scenario again and again. We see that the biggest enemy to our financial situation is compounding interest on credit cards, loans, lines of credit and mortgages, which makes us slaves to interest payments and keeps us from paying off principal. We're aware we should think about every dollar we spend and make an effort to "make the right decisions every day" to try to achieve our goals. Best of all, we know it's possible for anyone to become a millionaire over time (80% of millionaires are first-generation rich) with the right habits, strategies and willpower.

When you start saving, the amounts will seem small in the beginning, but over time, as you pay off loans (and don't take out new ones unless they are part of your wealth-building strategy), build equity in your home and reap the rewards of compound interest on savings and investments, you'll naturally find yourself thinking about accumulating and managing your wealth. What should you do with your savings? Where would they best be put to work? Should you buy an income property? Who should advise you?

Just being frugal and a great saver isn't enough; you'll need to become a shrewd money manager to make your financial dreams a reality. Good money management doesn't just happen—you have to make it happen by partnering with professionals whose skills you need and by taking some important preparatory steps.

partnering with
financial advisors

When it comes to managing your money, you are the best person to be in control of what is happening to your investments. However, there are many reasons why you might want some assistance:

- it can be a daunting task to try to oversee your own investment portfolio
- financial information at the company water cooler, in the newspaper or on the Internet may be old, biased or just plain far off the mark
- while we all have friends or co-workers who are happy to tell us about the stock they have that tripled and how they can help us do the same, chances are they are not so boastful about the three that tanked
- many of us simply do not have the time, the business background or the ability to study markets as well as someone who is a professional financial advisor

Admittedly, if you are concentrating on paying down debt, you may find you have limited funds to set aside in your investment nest egg. In the beginning, then, you should consider using forced savings (authomatic withdrawals) to allocate money for mutual funds (inside and outside your RRSP) with your local bank until you have amassed $20,000 to $30,000. As your investments grow, you may become ready for a professional to take a more hands-on approach and guide you as you manage your portfolio.

Andrew Cook is a partner with Marquest Investment Counsel Inc. in Toronto who manages individual accounts worth millions of dollars. He says you can approach most firms to get started with an investment plan; however, some organizations will expect you to bring $30,000, $50,000 or more to open an account. Cooks says, "Realistically you need a threshold amount of money to get appropriate attention."

Cook says that while the investment landscape can be quite confusing, it isn't rocket science, so you may not *need* a financial advisor. He says you should base your decision on whether you should hire someone to look after your portfolio on the amount of time you have available to monitor your accounts, your level of interest in following markets and, from a practical aspect, whether you have enough money to get proper attention from an investment advisor.

Once you have decided to hire a financial advisor, then you should interview two, three or more to find someone you are comfortable with. It's important to ask for references and actually check them. You will want to feel comfortable with them and be able to trust them.

> When interviewing an advisor, ask about their education, experience, investment philosophy, specialties, references, size of their client list, amount of an average client portfolio, and their disciplinary history.

A good financial advisor will be in the loop on current market trends and be aware of good investment opportunities before they become widespread public knowledge. They can also talk you out of risky investments that might be *hazardous to your wealth!* A financial advisor can steer you through the vast landscape of investment products and narrow them down to a list that is appropriate for you, your risk profile and investment goals. They can also offer advice and provide insight into longer-term trends in the markets.

But Cook says even when you have an advisor, the ultimate responsibility rests with you. "It is your money. You have to determine whether the advisor's advice is reasonable. If it does not make sense, don't do it. It should be easy to understand and make common sense. It can be intimidating given the different types of investment vehicles and the number of funds available, but I cannot emphasize strongly enough that common sense will help people make the right investment decisions," says Cook. If it does not make sense to you, and cannot be explained simply, it probably does not make sense and you should not do it. He insists, "There is simply no reason why you should buy something you cannot understand. There are enough [understandable] investment vehicles out there ... to help you achieve your goals."

When choosing any financial advisor you will want to know how they get paid. "Ask how the advisor is compensated to gain insight into their motivation. You ultimately want their interests aligned with yours," suggests Cook.

Financial Advisors Make Money Either:
- by the hour
- by flat fee
- by commissions on investment products sold
- through a percentage of assets managed on your behalf

Compensation is extremely important, so you should ask about any charges that you will incur when a purchase is made and when the investment is sold and if there are ongoing annual fees you are also responsible for. Advisors that charge a fee for advice don't make money by getting you to buy and sell something—theoretically they are more likely to act in your best interests because they don't make money from every transaction they recommend. The downside of this is that they may not have the incentive to follow your portfolio as closely as you may wish. Cook says, "Advisors that charge a commission may be more likely to pay closer attention to your portfolio because they only get paid when you do a transaction. The risk here is that the incentive to generate commissions may impair the objectivity of their advice." This is called churning accounts, and investors must be aware that when investments are being bought and sold within their portfolio there may be substantial charges being generated. The bottom line is to make sure that you know how your advisor is compensated and that you are comfortable following their instructions and suggestions.

Protecting Yourself

The vast majority of financial advisors are professionals operating with your best interests at heart; however, it is your money and you must be aware at all times what is happening with it. As Benjamin Franklin said, we must "oversee our own affairs with our own eyes and not trust too much to others. Trusting too much to others' care is the ruin of many."

The Small Investor Protection Association works to make people aware of how the investment industry operates, provide financial guidance, and fight for improved regulations, audit and enforcement to benefit investors. Stan Buell is the association's founder. Buell is concerned that many people working as "advisors" may have a conflict of interest because they are really no more than sales representatives selling financial products to generate commissions. Buell says, "The industry is misleading the public by saying that these people are financial advisors and investment consultants. The people working in the industry are pushed to sell certain investment products and they will do it whether it is good for the investor or not."

It's important that your advisor has you complete a know-your-client (KYC) form, which asks you all sorts of questions, from your age to how well you sleep when the markets become volatile. KYC forms are important to have so that your advisor clearly knows your investment knowledge, market experience, tolerance for risk, and financial goals. A younger person can afford to be more aggressive in their investment approach because they may be prepared to ride out the ups and downs of the market, while an older person should be investing more conservatively because they may need the money soon. Older Canadians have no need for risky investments and should never put savings at risk; savings are simply too hard to replace.

To protect yourself in the event of impropriety, ensure you have proper documentation of your relationship with your financial advisor. It's imperative that you receive monthly evaluations that show the value of your account, and they should be produced as a company standard, not as a handwritten or typed report. Problems often arise between investors and their financial advisors if much of their correspondence is verbal in nature, which can be difficult to track and hard to prove. Written statements will establish a paper trail of your transactions.

Never give power of attorney to an investment advisor because this will give the advisor full and complete access to accounts to trade, buy and sell at will. Ask questions and monitor your accounts and never assume your money is safe just because it is in the care of a financial advisor.

Buell has a special warning for people in small-town Canada, saying they need to be extra wary of slick financial advisors out to take advantage of people. "Don't deal with the little guy because any guarantees you are given are only as good as the person or company giving the guarantee. There are too many cases where small-time fraudsters take off with millions of dollars and then the money is gone and there is no chance of getting it back. Dealing with larger firms or bank-owned brokerage companies is not necessarily perfect, but in the event something goes wrong you will at least be able to get some of your money back," says Buell.

For more information on the Small Investor Protection Association you can visit its website at www.sipa.ca.You can also check out these websites for investing information:

Industry Canada's business and consumer site—www.strategis.gc.ca

The Investment Funds Institute of Canada—www.ific.ca

choosing
a lawyer

If you are lucky in life, you will require a lawyer for very few things. Hopefully, if you do it is to help close a profitable business deal, buy a house or deal with an inheritance left to you by a wealthy relative. Too often when you need a lawyer something bad is happening— you are either being sued, facing criminal charges or going through a divorce. None of these situations are pleasant and neither are the lawyer's bills that come with them.

Choosing a lawyer is one of the most critical decisions you will make. Unfortunately it's often a decision not made logically. Michael Reilly, of the Ajax law firm of Reilly D'Heureux Lanzi LLP, says, "Many people are referred to a lawyer by friends and family. This is a good start as you can receive feedback about the lawyer, but be careful. Unless the person giving you the referral works in the legal profession, his or her opinion about the legal ability of the lawyer is likely to be an uneducated one. Almost everyone thinks his or her own lawyer is the best. How else can one justify spending hundreds of dollars an hour?"

In addition to referrals, lawyers can be found through the Yellow Pages, the Internet and the Lawyer Referral Service (also listed in the Yellow Pages). Reilly says it's important to find a lawyer who has experience in the area of law you need. "You need to narrow your search to lawyers who practise primarily or exclusively in the area of law you require. Most lawyers restrict their practices to one or two main areas." While lawyers can practise in any area of law they choose, Reilly says that regardless of their experience, some lawyers will take a case in any area, learning as they go. He says, "Steer clear of these lawyers. You wouldn't want your family doctor to do your bypass surgery, so don't hire your real estate lawyer for your divorce."

> Having a lawyer on retainer is not necessary unless you are in need of legal advice on a regular, permanent basis. Generally you should call a lawyer only when you need one.

Reilly says that unless you are very wealthy, your choice of lawyer will likely be guided by what you can afford. "Although it is unlikely a lawyer will be able to accurately estimate the cost of your case over the phone, you can at least determine the hourly rate and narrow your list of potential lawyers according to your price range. A general rule, although certainly not accurate in every case, is the better the lawyer, the higher the rate." says Reilly. So how much should you expect to pay? Hourly rates range from $125 per hour to $500 per hour or more depending on years of experience, geographic location and the particular area of law. If your income is modest, you may qualify for Legal Aid. Except for criminal law, lawyers who accept Legal Aid certificates are often inexperienced. Reilly adds, "This is not always true, however, and many talented and experienced lawyers accept Legal Aid certificates." (You can check the Yellow Pages for the Legal Aid office closest to your home.)

After narrowing your list to three or four lawyers who practise in the area of law you need with hourly rates you can afford, you need to meet them. Reilly insists, "Do not hire the first lawyer you meet. You will be working closely with your lawyer for months and maybe years. You must be able to develop a working relationship." Reilly advises that you should comparison shop and gather information about each lawyer's experience. "Ask for an opinion on the merits of your case, strategies he or she might suggest, and the chances of success. An important question that is rarely asked is how many years the lawyer has been practising, and how many years were in the area of law you need." It's also a good idea to ask if the lawyer you are meeting with is the one who will be handling your file, because sometimes senior lawyers hand over cases to more junior lawyers. Reilly says, "This is not necessarily a bad practice, but you should know before it happens." Depending on the nature of your case, your lawyer may not be able to fully answer all of your questions; however, this is not an indicator of an inexperienced lawyer. "You should beware of a lawyer who seems too sure of the result and is more interested in discussing his or her retainer than your case. Most lawyers will expect you to be interviewing others and not pressure you to sign a retainer agreement and provide a cheque right away."

Many lawyers will offer a free initial consultation, but don't expect several free visits to go over your case. Confirm in advance that the lawyer's first visit is free or you could get stuck with a bill for your introductory meeting. Any lawyer to whom you are referred through the Lawyer Referral Service will offer a free 20-minute consultation.

Unfortunately, there are times when people have hired a lawyer only to find as their case proceeds that they have hired the wrong person for the job. If you feel you have, Reilly says, "Simply put, get a second opinion and, if necessary, fire the lawyer and get a new one. It is costly to change lawyers but the chances of success in your case decrease if you do not have full confidence in your lawyer's advice."

If you believe your lawyer has made an error, overcharged you or acted unprofessionally, consult another lawyer for an opinion. Your options include suing your lawyer, assessing his or her account with the court, and making a formal complaint. There are law societies in every province and territory in Canada that a lawyer must belong to in order to practise law there. You can check the Canadian Bar Association's website, www.cba.org, for more information on how to file a complaint, choose a lawyer or how to obtain legal aid in your area. For more information on Reilly's firm, visit www.reillylegal.com.

preparing
a will

As you save money, pay off debt and watch your equity and investments grow, you will want to ensure that you have a will so that your wealth is distributed to your loved ones as you would wish. Every adult Canadian should have a will, but for some bizarre reason half of us don't. Some of us may be paranoid that writing a will is a self-fulfilling prophecy: write a will one day and we'll drop dead the next. Others shy away from the expense of having a lawyer draw up a proper will, but it's money well spent for the family you leave behind. Having a will professionally drawn up, complete with powers of attorney (documents which give authority to others to look after your affairs if you're in a coma or for medical reasons unable to make decisions for yourself), costs about $250, or about $500 for a couple.

Why have a will? If you die without one, the law of the province where you live writes one for you. Each province has its own intestacy rules that provide a list of people who will inherit if a person dies without a will.

> You should update your will after important life events, such as a marriage, the birth of a child, a divorce or death of a spouse.

Inexpensive do-it-yourself will kits are available, but they are not recommended, especially if you have substantial assets. None of us really want to spend $250 to have a will drawn up, but if you have equity in your home, investments and prized possessions you want to leave to certain individuals, then a proper will is a must. A will kit can't offer advice and the one-size-fits-all approach does not take into account unique family situations. If mistakes are made and you're gone, the will is left open to interpretation and can be challenged in court.

You may also want to consider preparing a living will, which spells out your wishes as to the kind of care you want to receive after an accident, illness or when you are unable to speak for yourself and your condition is terminal. Some also refer to this as the "pull the plug" document. For more information on living wills, visit the website organized by the University of Toronto Joint Centre for Bioethics, www.utoronto.ca/jcb, which provides samples of living wills and instructional booklets, or call them at 416-978-2709.

For more information on wills, visit the Canadian Bar Association's website at www.cba.org.

Preventing a Family Fight

None of us like to think of our death, but having a will can prevent huge legal bills, stop bureaucratic red tape from tying up your estate and, most importantly, prevent family feuds when dividing up assets.

As much as parents may think their children won't fight when dealing with their estate, money does do strange things to people. No one knows this better than wills and estates lawyer Les Kotzer. He and Barry Fish of Fish and Associates in Thornhill, Ontario, have a law practice that tries to help people avoid family fighting over inheritances. Together they wrote the book *The Family Fight: Planning to Avoid It*. While it's important to have a will for many reasons, Kotzer says the main one should be the preservation of families. He became concerned after seeing a dramatic increase in family fighting among his clients. "It may be fighting that doesn't go to court and it's not over millions of dollars, but even when families fight over smaller things they end up no longer talking to each other and it can really lead to the destruction of relationships," says Kotzer. He adds, "I've had families throwing things in my office and yelling at each other, calling the people they used to walk to school with thieves and liars. Things can go downhill very fast."

Many people assume everything will go smoothly because family members love each other, but that's not always the case. Kotzer says, "Anybody who doesn't have a will would be very foolish to think this is the best way to leave a legacy for your family. If you don't have a will, there is a greater chance of a family fight. They may be fighting over this and that and there is nothing in place to guide the children on the distribution of your personal assets, anything to tell them how to divide up and your home and investments."

Family fighting is on the rise, partly because of the difference between the two generations. Kotzer sums it up this way: "There is a joke that goes, why did the baby boomer end up with one million dollars? It's because his parents left him three million." We are now experiencing possibly the greatest transfer of wealth between two generations, as the hand-off takes place from the thrifty Depression-era parents to their free-spending baby boomer kids. Kotzer elaborates, "The Depression-era parent was for the most part very wise. As a wills lawyer, I see the large amounts of money being passed down. They were more likely to save for a rainy day; … often they will come into my office and say that they have no debt—none! They have no mortgage, no loans and often no credit cards." The boomers are often another story. "What I'm seeing is the baby boomer, the ones that have a home, a cottage, expensive cars and expensive home theatre systems, now inheriting money from their Depression-era parents. While their mom and dad may have reused containers, clipped coupons and kept brown paper bags so they could use them again the next day for lunch, they are leaving their money to their children who are loaded with debt."

Unfortunately, many baby boomers are counting on an inheritance so they can pay down mortgage debt, car loans, lines of credits and credit card debt. People have high expectations that when their parents pass away, they will have a mattress to fall back on to pay off all the bills they have accumulated.

Problems arise when children find out there may not be enough money to go around. "Parents also make assumptions, such as, well, I'm sure if Billy needs money, Bobby will give it to him after I die." Kotzer says to never assume your kids are going to help each other financially after you pass away, because even though Bobby may have a great love for Billy, Bobby's wife may say, "You are not giving one cent to your brother because I can't stand him." Another factor is that people are living longer and the parents of baby boomers may need to spend their money to look after themselves. They will need medical care and money for nursing homes. They probably also didn't expect a lot from their parents because their parents didn't have much to leave behind for them.

Kotzer cautions that before involving lawyers in any family dispute, people should pull out old photo albums and review pictures that show siblings running on the beach, taking baths together or blowing out candles on a birthday cake. For more information check Kotzer's website, www.familyfight.com.

PART 4

INVESTING WISELY AND BUILDING WEALTH

Wealthy business people will tell you that "the first million was hard to make, but the next 10 million was a lot easier." This alludes to the fact that it is difficult to scrimp and save and invest your first few thousand dollars, but once you get started, have good habits and get the stock market and compounding interest on your side, it becomes a lot easier.

Having wealth to use in your favour is why the rich get richer. If someone has a million dollars and is able to get a 10% annual return on their investment, that's $100,000! This rate of return on investments is difficult to achieve in fluctuating real estate and stock markets, but it does show how wealth can be generated. Once you are able to put away tens of thousands of dollars, you too will be able to watch it grow in the various investment vehicles you choose.

Once you begin paying down debt, spending less than you make, and taking steps to prepare for wealth, you can begin setting aside money for the future and build the wealth you desire. You will see that a plan is necessary to help you manage your savings so you can benefit from compound interest, government tax incentives and the stock market. In the following chapters we will look at the power of forced savings when it comes to RRSPs and RESPs. We will address managing your mortgage so you can pay it off faster and give less money to the bank in the form of interest payments. We'll look at purchasing a second property, either a cottage or chalet or an income property.

As your savings and investments grow, so will your security and confidence. You will feel good about your financial position and know that you have money set aside to care for you and your family.

investing à la Andrew Cook

If you manage your own stocks and mutual funds, you may be playing the market with your fingers crossed. You should know there are many mistakes that novice investors make in their rush for big returns and easy money.

As mentioned in chapter 34, there are so many investments to choose from and different risk factors associated with them that you may find you require the advice of a professional money manager. It's common sense that a financial advisor, someone who spends every hour of the day following trends in the market and dealing with the world of finance, will have a better understanding of what the future may hold than the rest of us.

Once you have achieved a certain level of wealth, you will want to consider this step. Of course, even financial advisors have no crystal ball, but they can save novice investors from making common mistakes that unfortunately are made all too often.

Andrew Cook, whom we mentioned earlier in the book, is a partner in Marquest Investment Counsel Inc. based in Toronto. He is a portfolio manager who deals with individuals worth millions of dollars. Cook co-manages his company's funds with Gerry Brockelsby, Marquest's founding partner, and describes his role this way. "We are growth managers and manage money for institutions and high-net-worth clients. We are focused on absolute returns rather than beating a benchmark, such as the TSX exchange. Our funds have a performance fee structure, which aligns our interests with those of our unitholders and keeps us focused on absolute returns." In other words, if the clients make money, Marquest makes money—a win-win situation. So what can the average Canadian learn from a money manager like Cook who supervises millions of dollars within his investment company?

Do Diversify

Cook says one of the biggest mistakes investors make is not diversifying properly—"Either owning too much of a certain stock or fund as a percentage of your portfolio. While this can generate big returns, it can also generate big losses very quickly." We've all heard the saying, don't put all your eggs in one basket. This basic approach to investing makes sense at all levels, whether you are starting out or already a high-net-worth individual. Taking on unnecessary risk is really gambling with your investments, similar to spinning the roulette wheel at a casino. Cook explains, "It takes a long time or a big win to make up for big losses. In order to get back to even from a 50% loss, you have to have a 100% return. Investors must realize that investing is a marathon, not a sprint." Cook also says that while stocks are an important asset class, so are bonds and real estate.

Don't Chase Returns

Another common mistake made by the novice investor is "chasing returns"; in other words, investing in stocks that have already generated outstanding value. "There is a tendency for investments [that] have outperformed for a time to follow this with a period of underperformance. This can result in people putting money into assets at exactly the wrong time," warns Cook. In some cases, this mistake is compounded when the cash for new investment is raised by selling investments that have underperformed and are poised to outperform. "Chasing returns can also lead to lack of diversification because human nature tends to lead people to believe that investments [that] have outperformed are less risky. Investors can also fall prey to the greed factor, which can lead them to make bad investment decisions." Michael Douglas in the movie *Wall Street* may have said greed is good, but many an investor has lost a large percentage of their portfolio because they were greedy.

Do Know Yourself

Cook advises that investors review their current assets, risk tolerance and goals when making any and all investment decisions. What might be a great investment for your neighbour might be a terrible one for you. Remember, even when you have an advisor, the ultimate responsibility rests with you.

Don't Make Emotional Decisions

It's also human nature for investors to want to hold onto a stock that has dropped in value so they can at least break even when the stock rises to the price it was purchased at. The only problem is that it could take years for this to happen, so your money could be better put elsewhere. The other problem (as some investors know all too well) is that the stock may never return to the value it was purchased at or may becomes worthless. Thousands of investors held Bre-X stock, which skyrocketed only later to have no value whatsoever. Many investors who decided to take some profit when the stock was high did well. Others who held on until the end were left with worthless stock certificates. Cook says "Not selling when an investment is in a loss position and the fundamentals turn bad is another error many investors make."

Cook explains that it is normal not to want to sell at a loss, but that you are better to take your losses and keep the remaining capital to invest in something with positive fundamentals. He encourages investors to ask themselves this question: Would I be more upset if the investment continues to go down than I would be happy if it goes up? The answer is usually yes. It is psychology that keeps people in losing investments too long.

Cook says there are two reasons to sell: to prevent further losses and to improve the psychology of the investor. "Hanging onto bad stocks expends too much time and energy on negative events rather than focusing on finding positive investments."

Do Dollar-Cost Average

As this book will tell you several times, one of the best possible ways to invest for the future is forced savings. Whether money is direct-ed to a savings account or a stock plan, it's one of the easiest and most beneficial strategies. It is almost always better to invest over time than to try to make large investments all at once. "I think the best strategy is to invest money on a regular basis," says Cook. "This ensures that money is actually invested, rather than constant-ly postponing the decision. It becomes habitual. Additionally, you are not making a huge investment decision, which can be intimidat-ing—it can be done in small increments."

Do Pay Attention to Trends

The stock market is now not necessarily a "buy-and-hold stock market," and it is important to look at long-term trends. Cook says that different rules apply to different types of markets, and as these trends unfold they become accepted as common wisdom, because these trends last for 10 to 20 years. The "buy and hold" strategy, for example, works well in a long-term uptrending market, such as we were in from 1980 to 2000, but this is a recipe for underperfor-mance in a "sideways" trending market, such as we are in now and are likely to be in for the next five to 10 years. Suggests Cook, "In this environment, active management is required to generate above-average positive returns." Active management meaning watching stocks as they rise and fall and buying and selling as they move sideways through the market. This is when a money manager uses their experience to know when to get in and get out as stocks rise and fall.

Of course, no one has a crystal ball, but in what areas do Cook and his company believe there will be investment opportunities in the near future for investors? "We believe we are in an environment where commodity prices, e.g., oil and gas, copper, nickel, are in long-term uptrends [that] are likely to last for another five to 10 years. This is based on the increase in demand resulting from the industrialization of China, combined with lack of new supply coming as a result of underinvestment over the past 10 years due to a prolonged period of low commodity prices." Cook believes investing in this sector can be a good "buy and hold" strategy and that this area is likely to outperform over the next five to 10 years. He adds that "dividend-paying stocks as well as income trusts are likely to outperform over the next five years."

For more information on Cook's investment company, visit www.marquest.ca.

As I asked many experts for this book, I also asked Cook if there is any advice that stood out in his mind that he might wish to pass on to Canadians regarding saving or spending habits. He said that some friends recently told him about a deal on barbecues: if they all went in together and purchased several at once each person would save $500. So how much would the barbecues cost? Well, barbecues normally selling for $3,000 would only be $2,500. Cook declined his friends' offer. "I remembered the words of my father, Arthur Cook, who used to say, 'I guess we can't afford to save that much.'" Certainly it's a barbecue Cook could likely buy, but I guess he would rather spend less and put the difference into a good investment.

taking part in day trading

Day trading, or short-term investing, can be extremely risky. Day traders buy stocks and hold them for a few minutes, hours or days hoping to buy on a dip and sell on a spike. Too many people are gambling with their investment accounts or within their RRSPs. Some are risking money for their daily living expenses, home or retirement.

I have heard from viewers who are suicidal after investing a huge portion of their life savings into a single stock, hoping to double their money. One viewer told me he bought stock that immediately took a 25% drop. Rather than take a loss he held on, hoping it would come back, but it dropped again another 25%. He sold and lost half of his life savings. He said he couldn't bear to tell his wife what he had done.

Playing the market this way is the same as playing the slots at the casino: the odds are against you.

minimizing pricey fees for funds

If you are like many Canadians, chances are you have mutual funds in your investment portfolio. Whether they are inside or outside your RRSP, it costs you every year to hold mutual funds. Unlike stock holdings, mutual funds charge an annual fee to compensate the companies that manage them. Some mutual fund companies are charging big fees that are not always clear to investors. That's why you should know the "management expense ratio," or MER, of every fund you own.

Whether your fund is making money or not, you must still pay the MER—the percentage of your fund that will go to the mutual fund company annually. The size of the MER makes a huge difference in how much the fees will cut into your earnings. For example, if a mutual fund has an extremely low MER of just 0.18%, then on a $10,000 mutual fund the cost of holding the fund for three years is just $58. If a mutual fund has an extremely high MER of 3.1%, then on a $10,000 mutual fund the cost of holding it over three years would be $1,029. That's a huge difference.

You can find the MERs for a mutual fund by checking its prospectus or you can get the information online from the following websites and many others: www.globeinvestor.com, www.fundlibrary.com and www.morningstar.ca.

You may be getting more hands-on management with your fund if you pay a higher MER and higher returns, but that's not always the case. While most funds typically have MERs of about 1% to 2%, you should check every fund you own to see what the management fees are. If you have mutual funds through your bank or a broker, you can ask them what the MER is for your funds or check online through your bank or financial company's website.

If you do own funds with high MERs, you may want to monitor them closely and compare them to funds with lower MERs. If the lower MER funds are performing about the same, it may be worth making the switch to the funds with lower expense ratios.

If you're looking to buy a fund, a general rule is to avoiding buying "front-end load" funds, because for these you pay a sales commission up-front. Look for no-load funds and funds with low management expense ratios.

CHAPTER 40

benefiting
from RRSPs

By now, most of us know about the benefits of the Registered Retirement Savings Plan, or RRSP. Created in 1957 to help Canadians save for their retirement, RRSPs allow us to deposit money into a fund for our old age. For every dollar you put into an RRSP you get a tax break from the government. As your RRSP nest egg grows, it is sheltered from tax. It also encourages us to save for our retirement as we take on the burden of looking after ourselves.

The RRSP is generally regarded as one of the best tax shelters around, and when I interviewed personal finance expert Garth Turner, who was once Canada's Minister of National Revenue, he called the RRSP a must. Turner told me, "Canadians should view an RRSP like a large bubble where you can stack your financial assets. They are then free to grow and compound within the bubble, which shields them from taxes. Contributing just $100 a month can result in a quarter-million-dollar RRSP in just 25 years. It's the best leg-up on the future you are going to get!"

Investing in an RRSP makes good economic sense. At tax time the amount you have contributed to the plan is deducted from your taxable income, so chances are you will get a refund cheque. Your money grows in the plan sheltered from taxation and when you finally do need your money you roll your RRSP assets into a Registered Retirement Income Fund, or RRIF, which further defers taxes as long as you take out a minimal amount each year. Assets can be transferred to an RRIF at any time; however, all RRSPs must be converted by the end of the year in which you turn 69.

Generally, you can contribute 18% of your income. There is a maximum amount you can contribute of $16,500 for the year 2005. It's $18,000 for the year 2006 and indexed after that. The more money you make, the bigger the tax break you get. For example, if you contribute $5,000 in one year and are in a 40% tax bracket, you will get an immediate tax savings of $2,000. If you are in a 54% tax bracket, you will save $2,700. You immediately save money for your golden years.

It's hard to come up with several thousand dollars all at once, which is why contributing throughout the year, perhaps every month or every paycheque, is a good strategy. You can also load up your RRSP with any investment vehicles you want, such as low-risk GICs, savings bonds, mutual funds, stocks and small business shares.

> You may want to consider contributing to an RRSP plan for the spouse who is the lower income earner. You will get the same tax break as if you'd invested in your own name, but when the money is withdrawn it will be taxed at a lower rate.

It is now widely advised that if you don't have enough money to put in an RRSP you should borrow from the bank to make a contribution, but that's not true for everyone. It does enable you to get a refund cheque, which you can apply to the loan. If you do use your refund to pay off the loan, then borrowing money from the bank to put in your RRSP is a good idea. Unfortunately, most of us don't.

The government has changed restrictions on RRSPs so you can catch up on missed contributions; however, you cannot overcontribute more than $2,000 to your RRSP or you will be penalized.

So an RRSP is the best way to finance your retirement, then? Well, I have to admit that I have some concerns about RRSPs and the way the system operates. Here are a few of them:

- Have you talked to a retired person about their RRSP? That's when you hear them say, "RRSPs equal tax deferral—not tax savings."

- If you ever go to the bank to buy an investment property, the bank treats your RRSP as if it's not even there. It's like MC Hammer's rap song *U Can't Touch This*. If you want to use your RRSP to pay down debt, *U Can't Touch This!* If you want to take money from your RRSP for a home renovation, *U Can't Touch This!* If you are ever in a pinch and really need your RRSP money, you are taxed so heavily depending on your tax bracket and you can lose half of what you are taking out, meaning, you guessed it—*U Can't Touch This!*

- If the federal government ever becomes so cash-strapped that it's looking for money, it may not be able to control itself and may just tap into the billions of dollars of RRSP money that the baby boomers have saved up.

While almost every tax advisor says an RRSP investment is a great way to go, most add that this is if you reinvest your tax refund, which most of us don't. Another problem is that people may feel they are getting ahead by saving $10,000 a year in their RRSP but they continue to dig themselves $10,000 a year further into debt.

An RRSP is a great idea and I do believe it is a must for all Canadians to have some money in an RRSP, but what is most important is to have a balanced portfolio—money invested in an RRSP, money invested outside of an RRSP, real estate holdings, savings. I believe too many Canadians are putting too many eggs in the RRSP basket. They have tens of thousands of dollars there that they can't get at until they are over 65!

Granted, I would not want to dissuade anyone from saving money for their retirement, as we all should. Certainly anyone who does not have a company pension plan or someone who is self-employed should consider hefty payments to their RRSP. Many advisors say the tax break offered by the government is too good to turn down. I find that it is equally and perhaps more important to have money outside your RRSP and a plan to pay down debt. While RRSPs are part of a well-balanced retirement plan, debt reduction is just as important.

debunking financial myths

We've all heard that we need to have at least a million dollars to retire. While that is an excellent goal to shoot for, too many of us may be worried that if we don't have that much to fall back on we could be in serious trouble.

As the consumer advocate at CTV, I am pitched many books by many authors. A couple of years ago, one called *Smoke and Mirrors: Financial Myths That Will Ruin Your Retirement Dreams* came across my desk. It was unlike many of the self-help books of the day, as its message was that you don't need a million dollars to retire, you don't have to be in the stock market and you shouldn't borrow money to put in your RRSP.

The message from chartered accountant and author David Trahair was that Canadian banks and investment companies are using scare tactics to get Canadians to hand over their money. His take was that the more the banks can convince you that you need to borrow from them, the more money they can make off you in interest, fees and commissions. I did a story with Trahair at the time because many of the things he was saying seemed to make good sense. I interviewed him again for this book.

I think a lot of Canadians are as fed up as I am about a lot of the messages that come from these big financial conglomerates. I think people are worried about their retirement plans and I can understand why, because there are so many conflicting messages out there about needing millions of dollars to retire.

We've all seen the commercials during RRSP season about how you need $800,000 to $1.2 million to retire comfortably. It's this message that Trahair says gives people a sense of hopelessness.

The reality is that if people can get control over their finances and pay down their debt, the average Canadian will need nowhere near a million dollars in their RRSP to retire comfortably, which is good because the average Canadian is never going to get anything close to a million dollars in their RRSP. You would need to save $20,000 a year for over 30 years to build up that kind of portfolio. With the cost of living and raising children there's not too many Canadians that have $20,000 lying around at the end of every year.

Since everyone's personal finances are different, you may need a lot less than a million dollars; even $200,000 may be plenty to retire with. You have to think about what you want to do once you retire. If you plan to take an ocean liner to every seaport in the world, then you will need a lot more money than if you want to babysit your grandchildren and spend time gardening. Trahair says, "One of the seven habits of highly effective people is to begin with the end in mind, and unfortunately the majority of Canadians don't do that. They don't even think about their current state of finances, let alone what it's going to look like when they retire. If they did, they would increase their odds dramatically that their retirement would be comfortable or even better than their current situation is." You may be able to pull off a lifestyle of conspicuous consumption when you're earning a big salary, but it will be almost impossible to keep up your high-spending ways once you retire. You will either have to work longer or significantly cut back on your spending.

Trahair says that many financial elements change when you retire. You could be receiving money from a company pension plan, Old Age Security and the Canada Pension Plan. You likely may not be burdened with mortgage payments or have your children's education to worry about. You wouldn't have CPP and EI withheld from your income and you would probably be in a lower tax bracket so you would be taxed less. You wouldn't be putting any more money away for RRSPs; in fact, you'd be drawing money out. If your debt were paid off and you had control of your finances, you would find you need significantly less than you currently do.

> Getting rid of all your debt before you retire is key to needing less money at retirement. Trahair says, "The lack of a cash outflow is as good as, if not better than, a cash inflow." For example, suppose you have paid off your mortgage; your payments used to be $2,500 a month, but now that $2,500 a month isn't flowing out. If your mortgage is not paid yet and you still need $2,500 a month to pay it, you will have to take as much as $3,500 out of your RRSP because you will be taxed on it. Therefore your best bet is to have no debt at all in retirement.

There is a rule that is often quoted that says you will need 70% of your pre-retirement income after you retire to maintain your standard of living. That may be the right percentage for some people, but not for everyone. Trahair says, "In my case, since I track my finances and I project what our expenses will be after retirement, I believe we can maintain our standard of living once the kids move out and the mortgage is paid off on just 40% of what we are currently earning." This is just a minimum and of course we should try to save more; however, Trahair's plan can give you some peace of mind that you don't really need a million dollars or 70% of what you are currently earning to retire comfortably.

Trahair is also against the idea of borrowing money to put in an RRSP. "The banks have created a brilliant strategy by telling consumers they need to borrow money from them in order to top up their RRSPs. They loan you money and you immediately give it right back to them. They win on both sides of the ledger." Banks want to make money off your money. "If they can convince you that you are going to need a million dollars or more, then you are going to have to send them a heck of a lot of money and that makes them rich. The more you send them, the more they make."

He compares the banks to a large matching service. Trahair says,

> They take $100,000 from an older retired person and pay them 2% interest at the end of the year. They then turn around and find a younger individual and loan them that $100,000 for a mortgage and charge them 6% interest. The younger person is required to start paying the money back within two weeks and with payments top-heavy with interest so the banks are making a lot on that spread. My conclusion is that if the bank is winning, then who is losing? It's the people who are borrowing or investing with them.

Trahair says many investment houses want personal finance strategies to seem complicated so that they can say it's so difficult you won't be able to handle your finances but they will be happy to do it for you. He insists it's really not that complicated. "The key to getting your finances under control is very simple. If you spend less than you make every year, pay down debt and put money aside, then things will work out fine. If you spend more than you make every year, no strategy is going to save you."

The RRSP Trap

Now, I am not against RRSPs, and for the record neither is Trahair. However, a problem arises when people use RRSPs as their sole savings tool for their retirement. Trying to stuff as much money as you can into your RRSP is not only unnecessary, it could also hurt you down the road when you retire.

You get a tax deduction when you make an RRSP contribution, but it comes at a cost. The cost is that when you retire and start taking money out, you will be taxed at that point, so it is really a deferral of tax—not a savings of tax. While someone who borrows to put money in their RRSP can see a benefit if they immediately reinvest their tax refund, most of us don't. We just spend it on additional lifestyle things, like a more expensive vacation or a larger SUV.

"Even if someone's RRSP does well, there are problems with the RRSP at the end of the road," says Trahair. "When you turn 69 years of age you are required to convert your RRSP into a [registered] retirement income fund (RRIF) or annuity and the government then tells you how much you must take out each year, every year. There are minimal amounts that you have to take out, whether you need the money or not. That is one way that the government gets that tax refund back later on in your life." For example, currently, the minimal withdrawal amount is 7.38% in the year that someone is 72 years of age. If you had a million-dollar RRSP, you would have to take $73,800 out of your RRSP or RIF, whether you wanted to or not. Even if you had your finances under control and you didn't have a lot of expenses, you would still be forced to take that money out regardless and pay tax on it.

Trahair says there is another reason you don't want to have an excessive amount of money in your RRSP. "The second negative is that most Canadians have Old Age Security starting at age 65. It's the only free money you will ever get, but it starts getting clawed back once your income meets a certain amount and currently that's just over $59,000. So if someone actually had a million dollars and was taking $73,800 out of their RRSP, they would have part of that Old Age Security clawed back. It's money you deserve but wouldn't be able to get from the government."

The third reason that you don't want an RRSP loaded with cash is what happens at your death. When one spouse dies, the value of his or her RRSP or RRIF can go to his or her spouse tax free. But when the second spouse dies, the whole remaining balance of the RRSP and the spouse's RRSP goes on the final tax return of the second spouse to die. The government gets a huge tax grab at that point. Trahair cites an example. "The top tax bracket in Ontario is 46% and it kicks in at approximately $103,000 of taxable income. So if they had $400,000 left in their retirement income fund combined, approximately $300,000 of that is going to be taxed at 46%, so about $138,000 in tax will be owing on the final tax return." This might not make much difference to the person who is dying, but if they have children who they are passing their estate on to, it's a huge chunk to lose.

Clearly, there are negatives to building up a huge RRSP nest egg. If you already have a large amount of money in your RRSP and have concerns, raise this issue with your investment/tax advisor to see how you can try to limit the amount of tax you pay.

When I ask Trahair about the best advice he has ever received regarding personal finance, he quotes an article he once read. "I saw an article by John Templeton, the original Templeton, one of the best investors of all time, and the conclusion that he came to in this article was that the best thing that you can do, and this is from an investor, is pay off debt first. I couldn't believe that he would say something like that, but that's what he said, and that is what I would say. Pay off debt first. I would say if there is an enemy of personal finances out there, it's debt. You should try to have no debt. It's a simple philosophy that is easy to say, but difficult to do."

For more information on David Trahair's book, check out www.smokeandmirrors.ca.

setting up RESPs

One of the most important things parents can do for their children is to help provide them with an education, preferably college or university rather than the school of hard knocks. Young people who enter the workforce without an education beyond high school are forced into mediocre jobs with limited earning potential. According to Employment and Immigration Canada, jobs for people with only a high school education are disappearing, while jobs for workers with post-secondary education are tripling. And check out this statistic: a university graduate will earn $1,580,000 more in their lifetime than a high school graduate will. Employment and Immigration Canada says this amount could triple by the year 2015—just one more reason to tell your kids to stay in school. Even young entrepreneurs who want to start their own business should have a degree or diploma to fall back on in case their venture doesn't work out. Time in university or college is a great life experience, as well.

Two-thirds of new jobs require education beyond high school and tuition fees for courses can top $4,000 or $5,000 a year. Professional degrees for doctors, lawyers and dentists can cost as much as $12,000 to $15,000 annually. Add on the expenses of books, supplies, transportation, rent and other living expenses and you'll want to make sure you are socking some money away for your kids.

> The Canadian Bankers Association estimates that for a child that is three years old today, in 15 years, four years of education for a student living away from home could cost as much as $75,000 to $100,000.

While some subscribe to the theory that a student will work hardest in university if they are the one footing the bill for the cost of their education, with rising tuition and the added costs of attending school it is now almost impossible for even the most frugal student to save enough at summer jobs to pay for college or university. And many parents don't want to see their children step off the podium with a degree only to be saddled with tens of thousands of dollars in student loans as they prepare to enter the workforce. This is why a Registered Education Savings Plan, or RESP, is a must for all families.

The RESP program was created by the federal government to allow families to save up to $4,000 per year per child, to a lifetime total of $42,000 per child, in a tax-sheltered plan. The first $2,000 put in the plan is eligible for a Canada Education Savings Grant (CESG) of 20%. That means for every dollar you put in an RESP, the federal government will contribute 20 cents up to $400 per child per year. You can receive this grant of $400 a year for 18 years for a total of $7,200, which means the government is paying your child's first year of university for free! Families that earn $35,000 or less per year receive a bigger benefit. The government will match 40% on the first $500 saved in an RESP and 20% on the next $1,500 saved. This allows the family to receive a benefit of $500 annually. For a family earning between $35,000 a year and $70,000 a year, the government will match 30% on the first $500 saved and 20% on the next $1,500. This allows a $450 annual benefit.

The Lee family has decided to put $166.67 away every month for their child, and is considering both a non-RESP account and an RESP account. Here's what the accounts would look like after 18 years if both accounts had a compounded annual rate of return of 6%.

	In a Non-RESP Account	In an RESP Account
Principal	$36,000	$36,000
Interest earned after tax	$14,700 (tax rate of 40%)	$29,000 (tax sheltered)
Canada Education Savings Grant (CESG)	0	$7,200
Interest on CESG	0	$5,800
Total	$50,700	$78,000

As you can see, adding $400 a year from the government to the principal, and allowing it all to grow in a tax-sheltered account, the RESP account would provide the Lee family with $27,300 more for their child's education and it's free money!

Many families find it difficult with utility bills, mortgage and car payments to find extra money to put away for their children's education. When we see our children playing on the carpet or riding a bike, university and college seem so far off. But time flies and you will be pleased that you have put money away when it's time for them to take their high school graduation photo.

The easiest way to save is through our old friend forced savings. Having the money come straight out of your account every payday or every month is the easiest way to get an RESP started. This way, you also have the benefits of dollar-cost averaging over time (buying the investment as it fluctuates up and down). This, coupled with the free 20% education grant from the federal government, will have you well on your way to saving for your child's education.

With RESPs, the savings you set aside for your children grow tax free until your child is ready to go to any college or university in Canada or around the world (almost all private or trade schools are also eligible, but you may wish to check to make sure). The person putting money into an RESP does not get a tax deduction similar to that of an RRSP; however, since there is no tax benefit when the contribution is made, the contributions can be withdrawn tax free. Any interest, dividend or capital gains income earned on the money is taxable, but since students are essentially broke they would effectively pay little or no tax.

RESPs are offered through most financial institutions, such as your local bank, and anyone can contribute, grandparents, aunts and uncles and even friends. It is usually a good idea to have an RESP in a low- to medium-risk investment (such as a balanced mutual fund) because you would not want it to take a large dip when your child is ready to use it. Your local bank or financial advisor will be able to advise you which investment vehicle may be best depending on the age of your child.

What happens if little Johnny does not go to school? If your child does not go on to a post-secondary education you will either have to repay the 20% grant to the federal government, use the money for another child's education or donate the earnings from the plan to a post-secondary institution of your choice.

You can also create other savings programs in your children's names for their future, such as an informal trust. This is a regular, non-registered investment account set up for the purpose of investing funds for a child. The money is held in trust for the child until they reach the age of majority, at which time the child can use the money for anything—education, yes, but also backpacking through Europe, or a down payment on a condo.

By starting an RESP early, taking advantage of compound interest and using contributed dollars from the federal government, you can get an education nest egg growing for your child. As education costs continue to rise, planning ahead could give you peace of mind and help your family avert a financial crisis down the road when those big education bills start rolling in. It's working for our family and can work for yours, too.

participating in company stock purchase plans

Many workplaces across Canada have company stock plans that allow you to purchase shares in your company at a reduced rate. Employee stock purchase plans, or ESPPs, are a great way to purchase stock at a bargain, essentially buying your company on sale. Your bosses are hoping that by being a part owner, you will work hard to keep the stock price soaring. Some employers are more generous than others. The plan may allow you to buy three shares and get one free. Or it may allow you to spend $50 on a company stock and have it matched with $25. However it operates, taking part in a company stock plan is a no-brainer—it's free money! There are also stock bonus plans where an employer gives shares to an employee free of charge. Who wouldn't take part in that plan? Management positions may also be rewarded with "stock options," which give someone the opportunity to purchase shares at a predetermined price usually far below their market value.

> Because the money is deducted from your paycheque before you get a chance to see it and spend it, there is forced savings at work.

For whatever reason, some people who work for companies with stock purchase plans don't take part in them. They may feel they can't afford to or shy away because they don't fully understand how a company stock plan works. Well, find out! If you contribute $3,000 a year and your company matches you $1,000, you have added an extra $1,000 to your income.

Many of these plans will allow you to cash in your shares at any time; others allow you to cash in after a set period, such as one year. This means that even if you are trying to pay down debt, you can still make a stock purchase plan work for you. You can cash in the stock at the appropriate time and use the "free money" to pay down debt, or buy mutual funds or other stocks to put in your RRSP. If you have a self-directed RRSP, you may also be able to transfer your company stock right into your RRSP as is.

If the stock pays an annual dividend (a reward simply for holding the stock, which may range from 2% to 4%), your holdings will go up. Hopefully, over the course of the year the stock will also increase in value, but even if it doesn't you will be buying the stock frequently (usually every two weeks) as it fluctuates up and down, giving you the advantage of dollar-cost averaging. (Every two weeks you'll pay whatever the current market price is, whether it's $25, $23.50 or $26.) It's possible you'll have a lower average cost than if you'd made one lump-sum purchase. Here is an example of how it can work in your favour. If someone worked for Widget Company Inc. and the company discounted stock for employees by 25% here's how it would look after a year.

Offering date: 01/01/2006

Market price: $20/share

Employee purchase price: $15/share (with 25% discount)

If 200 shares are purchased in the first year: 200 shares x $15/share = $3,000

If at the end of the year, the market price is $22/share: 200 shares x $22/share = $4,400

This equals $1,400 free for the employee!

Of course, the stock price could drop as well, but even if it does you will be buying stock at the reduced price and your company will still be matching it with a free 25%.

A good ESPP strategy is to use any raise you receive to increase the amount you contribute to your stock plan. Although most companies have a limit as to what they will match (such as up to 10% of your salary), you may still be allowed to buy extra stock, and since the plan is already set up, why not take advantage of this forced savings strategy?

There is one very strong warning I would give about company stock plans and that is that at some point *you must diversify!* You do not want to be holding too much of your company's stock if it goes into a slump, and especially if it takes a permanent nosedive on the markets. A good example of this is what happened to thousands of Americans who had invested heavily in Enron through their company stock purchase plans. Many saw their investments dwindle from half a million dollars to next to nothing. Their shares became practically worthless. You should never have 100%, 50% or even 30% of your savings in a single stock, whether it's your company's or not. No more than 10% of a retirement account should be in any one stock. So, as your holdings increase, sell some company stock and put the money into blue-chip stocks, bonds or other investment vehicles.

You should always take advantage of any offering by your employer that will increase your bottom line. Being part of the company stock plan is a great way to do that. If your company has one and you feel you can't afford to be part of it, consider this: you can't afford *not* to be.

owning (not renting) your home

One of the most important steps you can take to secure your financial future is to buy a home. Early in life we have to rent rooms, apartments or housing for schooling or a first job, but the goal should be to get into a home and stop paying rent as soon as possible. You simply cannot get rich renting. You just can't.

I know someone who is a lifelong renter. He has "talked the talk" about buying a home, but enjoys his twice-yearly holidays and high-tech toys too much to save up a down payment. He told me recently that a house he had considered buying 10 years earlier had gone up in value nearly $100,000. He would have bought it, should have bought it and could have bought it, he said, but he didn't. Now he's been told the rent for his apartment is going up to $1,200 a month.

He's been renting for 20 years   20 years x $1,200 a month = $288,000

If he rents for another 30 years   30 years x $1,200 a month = $432,000

For $720,000, he could have a nice house!

Renting makes the landlord rich and keeps you poor. Why would you want to pay off someone else's mortgage when you could be paying off your own? There is also something empowering about owning your own home. There is peace of mind and security knowing you own real estate and no one can evict you from your living space.

Owning a house is a great forced savings plan because you have to make those payments to keep your mortgage in good standing—and you will. The first year or two of home ownership can be trying as you get used to mortgage payments, utility bills and taxes but it gets easier.

There is a double benefit that renters never see: as you pay your home off, it also increases in value. Over time real estate has always gone up. There have been dips in the real estate market in the early 1980s and the early 1990s, but over the long haul housing has always increased in value. The last 10 years in Canada has seen many homes rise in price by 30%, 50% and in some markets 100%. Imagine buying a home for $200,000 and having it increase in value to $300,000, or buying a $300,000 home and watching it increase in value to half a million dollars. A $200,000 increase is something a renter will never see. Housing prices over the past five years have seen annual increases of 4% to 9% depending on your location in Canada.

Will the real estate bubble burst? There is no doubt the housing market will eventually have to cool down after the overheating that's making housing prices skyrocket (you should see what a million dollars gets you in Toronto these days). But no one expects a huge slide in prices on the scale of what happened in 1982 or 1992. And you have to live somewhere, right? Over time a home is the best possible investment you can make.

managing your mortgage

A home is the largest investment most of us will make, so negotiating a mortgage is one of the most important financial decisions we are faced with. Managing your mortgage wisely over time can save you tens of thousands of dollars and see you pay off your home years earlier than if you took a hands-off, pay-it-and-forget-it approach. Often when you go in for a mortgage the bank automatically qualifies you for the 25-year amortization and doesn't bother to explain all the money-saving options available to you so they can keep you locked in as long as possible. It's important that you make the best decisions regarding interest rates, scheduled payments, additional payments and mortgage terms.

Interest Rates

Keeping track of your mortgage and interest payments is now easier than ever to do with the financial software available and the mortgage interest calculators provided on the Internet. Most major banks have mortgage calculators on their banking websites (they just don't always make them easy to find). You can plug in your mortgage figures to see how much you're paying in interest along with the principal you've borrowed. The amounts can be shocking, and it's this surprise that's a sign that you should try to completely understand how calculating your mortgage works.

Calum Ross, senior vice-president with The Mortgage Centre–Mortgage Professionals Inc. in Toronto, says, "The average consumer does not feel comfortable sitting across from their banker playing hardball and negotiating a lower interest rate. In fact, once you're in a mortgage product, the natural Canadian tendency is to forget about it. It comes out of your account every week, biweekly or monthly and unfortunately people don't get involved in the act of monitoring their mortgage." He continues, "Most people want to get the best interest rate, but in practice people want to save the most money and there are different mortgage products available that can help you do that." For an example of how negotiating even half a percent less can save you tens of thousands of dollars review chapter 23, Understanding Interest Rates.

Shorter Amortization

The most obvious way to save money is to pay back your mortgage as soon as you can. By just paying a few hundred dollars more a month, you can pay off your home five to 10 years earlier! Suppose Surjit and Jasmine buy a house and need a mortgage of $322,000. Let's say they negotiate an interest rate of 7.5% and agree to amortize the mortgage over 25 years.

$322,000 mortgage at 7.5% interest rate over 300 months = monthly payment of $2,356

Total amount of interest paid to the bank over the term of the mortgage = $384,680

If Surjit and Jasmine made an effort to pay the money back in 20 years they would save considerably.

$322,000 mortgage at 7.5% interest rate over 240 months
= monthly payment of $2,572

Total amount of interest paid to the bank over the term of
the mortgage = $295,159

Surjit and Jasmine's monthly payment would go up only
$216, but they would save $89,521 in interest payments and be
done with their mortgage five years sooner! Let's see what the savings would be if they tried to pay it back in 15 years.

$322,000 mortgage at 7.5% interest rate over 180 months
= monthly payment of $2,964

Total amount of interest paid to the bank over the term of
the mortgage = $211,530

Surjit and Jasmine's monthly payment would go up another
$392, but they would save another $83,629 in interest payments
and be done with their mortgage in 15 years. I'm aware you would
need a good income to make these kind of mortgage payments, but
it does show how a shorter amortization period dramatically
reduces your interest charges.

Accelerated Biweekly Payments

Making accelerated biweekly payments (every two weeks) is an
excellent strategy because you will make 26 payments in a year
instead of 24. This allows you to make one extra payment a year
that you wouldn't make if you were paying monthly (and you won't
even miss it). The savings are similar to that of a shorter amortization period. By matching biweekly mortgage payments to your paycheque, you don't end up searching for money at the beginning of
each month. Using Surjit and Jasmine's example of a $322,000
mortgage with an interest rate of 7.5% and a 25-year amortization
illustrates the savings that accelerated biweekly payments can have.

$322,000 mortgage at 7.5% interest rate over 300 months = monthly payment of $2,356

Total amount of interest paid to the bank over the term of the mortgage = $384,680

However, if they make accelerated biweekly payments ...

$322,000 mortgage at 7.5% interest rate = biweekly payment of $1,178

Total amount of interest paid to the bank over the term of the mortgage = $296,169

The amount they pay every four weeks remains the same as their monthly payment of $2,356. But the extra payment each year makes a huge difference. In this case the mortgage would be paid back in 20.2 years, almost five years sooner, and they would have saved $88,511 in interest payments.

Lump Sum Payments

It's not always possible to put an extra "lump sum payment" on your mortgage, but those who do will see their mortgage paid off substantially faster and save tens of thousands of dollars in interest. Let's use Surjit and Jasmine's example once again.

$322,000 mortgage at 7.5% interest rate over 300 months = monthly payment of $2,356

Total amount of interest paid to the bank over the term of the mortgage = $384,680

Now, assume that Surjit and Jasmine are able to put a lump sum payment of $1,000 a year, every year, on their mortgage. Doing this would allow them to pay off their mortgage in just 22 years and 10 months and pay $343,923 in interest—a savings of $40,757. I prefer the accelerated biweekly plan because it is like forced savings and once it's set up you have to make the payments.

Saving an extra thousand dollars a year can be difficult to do; however, if you could combine an accelerated biweekly payment approach with lump sum payments you would be well on your way to owning your own home even faster.

Additional payment features may be available to you. Some lenders now offer a 20/20 prepayment option. This allows you to increase your payments by 20% or pay off up to 20% of your original balance each year. There may also be a match/miss payment option. This allows you to match one or more of your payments and miss one at a later date for each matched payment within the term. In some cases, the bank will have set limits on the number or size of additional payments you can make each year, or they may only allow you to make the payment on the anniversary date you signed your mortgage, which may be a time you don't have extra money handy. Whatever you do, you should be asking your mortgage holder what options are available to you to pay down your mortgage faster.

Mortgage Term

As well as deciding how many years you will take to pay back your mortgage you must also decide how long you plan to lock in for. Historically, homeowners save money when they sign up for short-term mortgages. Ross says, "Just as we know over the long run that stocks will outperform bonds, which will outperform money markets, we also know that there are benefits to short-term and variable-rate mortgages. The real philosophy to save money is to go one year or go variable." Ross says homeowners should know that "people in the mortgage industry get paid more the longer the term you go with."

Not everyone can handle the stress of going short term, especially if they have a large mortgage and they're cutting their payments close. They may feel they can't afford to, but the truth is they can't afford not to. Ross says, "Some people don't have the stomach for variable-rate mortgages. However, we know that 88% of the time over the past 30-year cycle ... someone is going to save an average of $22,000 in interest per $100,000 borrowed on a 20-year repayment." The problem with short-term mortgages is that a hike in interest rates can have some mortgage holders concerned interest rates are going to spike and that's when they panic and lock in for the long term. Ross calls this myopic loss aversion. He says, "Myopic loss aversion, in layman's terms, is that most people have long-term intentions; however, when something changes in front of them, they all of a sudden act like a deer in the headlights."

Consumers who buy into a five- or seven-year mortgage are really paying extra for peace of mind. It's really like mortgage insurance, which can be expensive. "What a longer-term or fixed-term product really is giving you over a shorter-term mortgage, no matter which way you slice it, is peace of mind. It's peace of mind against the interest rate going up for a longer period of time. People buy insurance to share risk. And really what you are doing is paying extra to cover yourself against interest-rate risk," says Ross. Taking a long-term mortgage could also see you paying huge penalties if interest rates drop and you want out of your mortgage. (I will discuss this in the next chapter.)

As you pay down your mortgage you should also be thinking about what do to with the equity that is building up in your home. Ross says, "You should be looking at taking any equity and putting it into investment vehicles that will allow you to deduct interest. The key is to channel non-tax-deductible debt to become tax-deductible debt." If you borrow to invest, the interest you pay is tax deductible. For example, if you took $50,000 from your home's equity to buy mutual funds and the bank charged you 5% interest annually, you would pay the bank $2,500 a year in interest charges. But since you borrowed to invest, the entire $2,500 is tax deductible. Once you start paying down your home, this is an option you may wish to explore with your financial advisor or banker.

When you renegotiate your mortgage you should always try to keep your payments the same as before. If the interest rate drops there may be a temptation to make smaller payments so you will have the extra cash left over to spend. Resist this temptation if you want to pay down your mortgage faster. If you remortgage and move to an interest rate of 5.5% from 6.5%, you should keep your mortgage payments the same. If you don't and spend that 1% interest savings you will not be paying down your principal as fast as you could if you left your payments as they were.

You should also resist the temptation to skip a payment when the offer is made by your bank. It's pitched as a way to give you more spending money around the holidays, but it's just another way banks try to get more interest payments out of you in the long run.

We need to be more proactive in our mortgages. For online mortgage calculators and more information, check out www.calum-ross.com. You should also look at your lending institution's website to review what mortgage payback options are available to you so you can try to become mortgage free faster.

CHAPTER 46

breaking your mortgage

When you lock into a five-, seven- or 10-year mortgage for "peace of mind" you may think you are further ahead in case interest rates go up, but what if they drop? If interest rates go down, you are locked into a mortgage with a higher rate than what the market will currently give you.

This is when you have to calculate if it's cheaper to break your current mortgage agreement and pay a penalty to the bank, or ride out the mortgage payments until your term is up. Some consumers mistakenly believe you can get out of your mortgage by paying a three-month interest penalty, but that is not the case. You have to pay three months of interest or the interest rate differential, whichever is greater. The interest rate differential penalty can be quite high; however, in some cases it may be worth paying a penalty to take advantage of lower rates.

The interest rate differential is a penalty for early prepayment of all or part of a mortgage outside of its normal prepayment terms. This is usually calculated as the difference between the existing rate and the rate for the term remaining, multiplied by the principal outstanding and the balance of the term. It sounds complicated, but what it means is if you want to break your deal with the bank they are going to stick you with a huge financial penalty.

Mortgage holders really need to understand when it makes sense to break a mortgage to get a better rate and when it makes sense to stick with the rate you have. Calum Ross, of The Mortgage Centre–Mortgage Professionals Inc., says, "The people who refinance the most in this country are six-figure income earners. These people have the financial knowledge and advisors who can crunch the numbers to let them know when it makes sense to refinance."

As soon as there is a spread of more than 1% interest between what you are paying and current rates and you have more than one year left on your mortgage, you should consider paying a penalty to get out of it. "I have a client who locked in for 10 years." "His cost to break his mortgage was $17,000. This is an uncomfortable figure to be sure. However, the truth of that matter is he will save $40,000 over the next nine-and-a-half years."

If you have locked in, you need to do the math to see how much you will save and whether it's worth getting out of your existing deal with your lender. Ross says, "It's really not about the penalty and that cost can look horrific. It's about the savings. You've got to run the math." Here is an example of how a lender will calculate the penalty.

> Amanda has a mortgage of $100,000. She is paying 8% and there are three years left on her five-year term. Her outstanding balance is $97,218. Amanda is considering breaking her mortgage and taking out a new one at the 6% interest rate currently being offered. Amanda would have to pay a penalty based on three months' interest or the mortgage differential, whichever is higher.

The three-month interest penalty equals
Outstanding balance x monthly interest rate of Amanda's mortgage x 3 months =
$97,218 x (8% ÷ 12 months) x 3 months = $1,944
The three-month penalty equals $1,944.

To figure out the interest rate differential, we take the interest rate on Amanda's mortgage (8%) minus the current market mortgage rate (6%).

8% - 6% = 2% (interest rate differential)

The interest rate differential penalty equals
Outstanding balance x monthly interest rate differential x months left on mortgage =
$97,218 x (2% ÷ 12 months) x 36 months = $5,833
The interest rate differential equals $5,833.

If Amanda wanted to break the mortgage she would have to pay a penalty of $5,833 since it is the higher of the two calculations. So would it be worth it?

If she stayed with her current mortgage with a 15-year amortization:
$97,218 mortgage x 8% x 36 months = monthly payments of $929.07
interest paid over three years = $22,057
mortgage remaining after three years = $85,829

If Amanda took a new mortgage with a three-year term at 6% with a 15-year amortization:
$97,218 mortgage x 6% x 36 months = monthly payments of $820.38
interest paid over three years = $16,383
mortgage remaining after three years = $84,068

What does all this mean? Well, if Amanda decided to pay the penalty of $5,833 she would save $5,674 in interest and her mortgage would be $1,761 less with the lower rate. Amanda would save about $1,500 by breaking her mortgage and going with the lower rate.

If you are locked in and wonder if you should break your mortgage, you can always talk to your bank or lender. Ross says, "You also want to ask them if there is any possible way to minimize the penalty amount that you have to pay." You may be able to make a lump sum payment or "blend-and-extend" your current mortgage rate with a lower rate. By combining your higher rate with a lower one you can take advantage of lower rates without having to pay a penalty.

Things to Remember When You Switch Banks or Break Your Mortgage

- A penalty may apply if you wish to switch institutions before the end of your mortgage term.

- You may have to pay legal fees to discharge the old mortgage and register the new mortgage.

- Other administration fees may also apply.

- Don't hesitate to ask the lending institution whether it is willing to pay part or all of these fees. If not, ask yourself if the savings of going to a new institution are greater than the cost of switching.

- If you initially received a discounted rate, the financial institution may apply this discount to your current mortgage rate.

- If you received a "cashback" instead of a discounted rate, you may have to reimburse a portion (or all) of the cash you received.

You will never be faced with paying a huge penalty or have to worry about the interest rate differential formula if you go with short-term mortgages no longer than a year or two. But if you have locked into a long-term mortgage and interest rates have dropped, you should investigate if you can save money by paying a penalty to get out of it.

considering reverse mortgages

If you are an older Canadian whose home is entirely paid for, you may be intrigued by reverse mortgages after hearing commercials about them. Reverse mortgages are a way to stay in your home as long as you want while at the same time receiving payments from a reverse mortgage company. Sounds great, but before embracing this concept it's important to know exactly what you are signing up for.

With a regular mortgage, a bank lends you money, you make payments and eventually you own your own home. The opposite is the case with a reverse mortgage. You own your own home, you receive payments, but in the end the reverse mortgage company can own your home or at least a substantial part of it. Reverse mortgages may be ideal for someone who has no children or dependants and plans to spend every last breath in their current home. However, even though many of us think we would like to be in our own home forever, no one knows what the future holds; you may not be able to manoeuvre stairs or cut the grass as you get older.

A reverse mortgage allows homeowners to turn the equity in their homes into cash without having to sell their house. The concept is aimed at people who have paid off their homes and own them outright. There is then money to enjoy in retirement, no repayments are required during your lifetime, you can stay in your family home and the proceeds you receive are tax free.

The disadvantages? A reverse mortgage can eliminate your home equity. Repayment to the reverse mortgage company is due upon selling of the home or your death. The longer you belong to a reverse mortgage plan, the more equity is depleted from your home. This can take away from any inheritance that you plan to leave your heirs. If you have children, you would be far better off telling them you are considering a reverse mortgage so they can help you decide if there is a better option. Too often, parents move ahead with a reverse mortgage without their children knowing about it.

Be very cautious about signing a reverse mortgage and consider lines of credit, home equity loans or other options before locking into a plan that depletes your equity rather than increases it.

using the equity in your home to buy real estate

The first piece of real estate you should own is your home. If you can buy a home for $100,000 and sell it for $400,000 and you won't have to pay a penny in capital gains because it is your principal residence. It's really the best financial move you can make.

Once you have a home and start paying down the mortgage it will also (depending on current market conditions) begin appreciating in value. Before long, you will have equity in your home that could be used for other things, such as purchasing other real estate.

There are many different ways to make money in real estate and various formulas for achieving it. You could purchase a recreational property, rental property or simply create a basement apartment in your home.

Douglas Gray is the author of *Making Money in Real Estate* and is an authority on ways that Canadians can make real estate investing work for them. Gray agrees that first and foremost, owning your own home is the best way to get into the real estate market. "Seven out of 10 Canadian millionaires have made money in real estate and many of those just did it with their own principal residence that they bought at the right time at the right place. They had a long-term hold and before they knew it, they were sitting on a million dollars worth of real estate."

While most of us see the obvious benefits to home owner-ship, the majority of Canadians do not move beyond owning more than a single property. Gray says, "It's fear of the unknown but people should realize there are ways you can get into real estate grad-ually so you have total comfort and very minimal risk."

According to Gray, there are 10 reasons to invest in real estate in Canada.

1. **Attractive return on investment**. Historically, real estate has increased in value greater than inflation and many other forms of investment.

2. **Tax advantage**s. There are many tax breaks, including writ-ing off loan interest on investment properties or rental suite income against a portion of your home-related expenses.

3. **Low starting capital using the principle of leverage**. Using a small amount of money and borrowing the rest (using other people's money) is an excellent investing strat-egy. Many people have become millionaires by applying this principle.

4. **Low risk**. Any investment has risk and you can lose money in real estate, but Gray says the reasons people lose money are well-known and can be avoided when applying proven principles.

5. **Appreciation**. Even with dips, slumps, highs and lows, the national average for real estate in Canada has increased in value 5% each year, every year, for the past 25 years.

6. **Equity build-up**. As you make payments on your mortgage, you are paying down the principal. As you reduce debt, you build up equity.

7. **Inflation hedge**. Over time, land appreciation has been 3% to 5% greater than inflation.

8. **Increasing demand for land.** You know what they say about land: they're not making it anymore. With population increases, immigration and the decreasing supply of land, prices will continue to rise.

9. **Part-time involvement and flexible options**. Investing in real estate does not require more than part of your time.

10. **Real estate investing skills can be learned**. Compared to other investments, buying and selling real estate is a relatively straightforward process. Anyone can learn the basic fundamentals of real estate and with research avoid the classic pitfalls.

Before you decide to dive into a real estate investment, you have to determine the kind of property owner you want to be. Gray says you have to analyze the kind of person you are and what it takes for you to sleep soundly at night. "You have to know yourself really well. Are you debt averse or not? If you are, you are going to have trouble with leverage, which is very important when you invest in real estate. Secondly, do you want to manage [the property] yourself or do you want someone else to manage it for you?" Then you have to research what is out in the marketplace and decide on the areas that interest you. Are you going to buy a condo, a townhouse or apartment? Maybe you want to buy a recreational property or a cottage lot. When you have a clear focus on the kind of real estate you are interested in, you need to also examine your debt threshold level, both psychologically and financially. You will need to look at what skills you bring to the investment property and how much time you have available. Gray says equally important is knowing what your long-term or short-term hold period is.

Buying another home, condo, duplex or multi-unit building can be a way to accumulate wealth quickly, but it is not without its challenges. That being said, we have all heard of the successful businessman who purchased one two-unit building and then used the equity built up in that property to buy another one, and then another one, and so on. It can be done (I know someone who has done it).

Gray says, "You have to define yourself and what kind of commitment you are prepared to make or able to do. If you have a busy life you might not be able to deal with landlord-tenant issues, which is why you may want to have a property management company look after the property, select the tenants and do the maintenance." A property management company may take 10% of the monthly rent to look after the property for your peace of mind. Or you may want to do it yourself. Either way, you would select the property based on the same sound principles that you would to choose your own home to ensure it is likely to increase in value and will be attractive to another buyer when you go to sell it.

Buying Investment Property When a Child Attends College or University

Buying a condo, townhouse or other residential unit for a student heading off to college or university for three to five years is an excellent way to get yourself into an income property (and give your child an education in real estate at the same time). If your children are heading off to university, they are going to have to live somewhere, and this may be an opportunity for you to buy a place for them to stay. Gray says, "Parents who have children going to university for four years may think, why shouldn't I buy a condo or apartment unit for my child while they attend school? If there is another child coming up behind them, the unit could be in the family for four, six to eight years." If the unit is in the family, parents can have an expectation that it will be looked after reasonably well. It will also save you money because you would otherwise be paying rent for other accommodations you don't own anyway. Gray says, "Over time you will get capital appreciation. It's an excellent investment and a lot of parents are doing it."

There are pitfalls, though, and one of the most important considerations is deciding whose name will be on the property—your child's or yours. If you have the property under your child's name, then they get the capital gain benefit tax free because it's their principal residence. If you put it in your name, then it's an investment and you may have to pay tax on a capital gain, but you can write off any interest you are paying because it's an investment property. Gray says, "The risk of putting it in your children's name is that they could make an imprudent decision that may affect the value of the property. For example, they might cohabit with a partner and then it doesn't work out and the partner says [they] want a cut of the action on the property." There could also be debts that attach themselves to the property because utility bills weren't paid or maintenance fees were in default. Gray says, "If the parents are putting up the money and they are holding the mortgage, then it is they who should have their name on the property to protect themselves."

If it's a house that you purchase, you or your child can rent it out to three or four other students. That can actually get cash flowing in that can help pay down the mortgage. You will also have the upkeep of the house to worry about, such as cutting the grass, shovelling the snow and changing the furnace filter. If it's a condo, there will be maintenance fees but the basic maintenance will be looked after. You have to weigh the pros and cons.

Choosing a Property

Over time a home will increase more than a condominium in value because of the land it sits on. Like with any investment decision you will have to research the geographic area. Is it in an attractive area for the things that are important to you, like safety, transportation and shopping for necessities? Call the local police department to ask about crime and crime statistics in the area. You will want to ensure you feel comfortable if you are going to have two daughters living on their own five hours away from you. Also, is the property likely to be worth more when you plan to sell it? Will others see the same opportunities that you did? There is no such thing as easy money and your child may have to worry about her roommates not paying the rent instead of concentrating on her studies. Still, if you have accumulated equity in your home and your children have to live somewhere for a set period of time when they attend school, it is an option that should be considered. It could pay off nicely and give your child a lesson on the value of property ownership. For more information, check out Gray's website at www.homebuyer.ca.

Renting Out a Portion of Your Home

Renting out the basement of your home is one way to segue into the landlord business. This may be ideal for someone who has been a lifelong renter and is only now jumping into the housing market. Purchasing a home that is already set up for a basement apartment or can easily be converted to one (via a side entrance or separate entrance) is an option for someone who would be able to rent out the basement (or even the top floor of the house) to a tenant to help pay the mortgage payments until they can afford the house they really want. An extra $600 a month from a tenant will go a long way toward paying the mortgage. You might also want to try to keep the property as a secondary rental property when you move out. Renting out a portion of your home may also be an option for a retired person who is looking to generate extra income. You should check with local bylaws concerning the law regarding basement apartments in your municipality, although Gray says, "the reality is that people do it whether they are bylaw compliant or not."

---

purchasing a cottage or chalet

Cottage and chalet prices have skyrocketed over the past decade as baby boomers looking for a place to unwind, relax and listen to the loons have gone on a buying spree. With waterfront lots becoming scarce, some investors are taking to the ski hills to buy chalets or even to the countryside to buy hobby farms.

Real estate prices continue to experience double-digit increases in many markets across the country. Supply and demand is driving up prices—for every seven people looking to buy a cottage, only two cottage owners plan to sell within the next three years. The price hikes are likely to continue. Here's what the Royal LePage *Recreational Property Report 2005* on waterfront cottages found across Canada.

Recreational Property Price Summary
Standard Land Access Waterfront Properties (*Average Price by Province*)

Province	2004	2005	% Change
Prince Edward Island	$115,000	$119,375	3.8%
New Brunswick	$79,375	$84,375	6.3%
Nova Scotia	$147,000	$146,500	-0.3%
Newfoundland	$47,500	$53,000	11.6%
Quebec	$328,667	$412,500	25.5%
Ontario	$327,574	$351,212	7.2%
Manitoba	$204,167	$262,500	28.6%
Saskatchewan	$150,000	$157,500	5.0%
Alberta	$500,000	$625,000	25.0%
British Columbia	$135,125	$144,575	7.0%
National Average	**$203,441**	**$235,654**	**15.8%**

A cottage or recreational property can be a wise move in life because you will be able to enjoy it as a secondary place to spend quality time, and it will almost definitely increase in value. Hindsight is 20/20, but anyone who already purchased a cottage or has one in their family has seen it increase in value tens of thousands or even hundreds of thousands of dollars.

Many people may feel that they have missed their chance to buy cottage property but it could still be a good investment opportunity, according to Douglas Gray author of *Making Money in Real Estate*. He says, "If there are properties that you are interested in that are in high demand because of their proximity to major cities, they may be unaffordable to you. So what you should do is go farther. Maybe it's a three- or four-hour drive instead of a two-hour drive. The farther out you go the less expensive it's going to be and it may then be within your affordability. Besides, within five years people are going to be moving farther out anyway so your property will increase in value." Gray recommends that you go to a less well-known lake, instead of a better known lake if that's what it takes to get a cottage property that you can afford. Aside from personal use, he says, you should always be thinking about resale.

Real estate has been so hot in some areas of the country—whether it's Shediac, New Brunswick; Haliburton, Ontario; Cranbrook, Alberta; or Hatheume Lake, British Columbia—that some worry that the real estate bubble could burst, but Gray is optimistic even for someone considering cottage properties today. "If you take a look at the big picture of real estate in Canada over the past 40 years, real estate across the board has averaged 5% growth a year, every year. There might be cyclic periods when there is a slump, but you know it will go back up and eventually [be] higher than it was before. We've seen this historically and cyclically. In that sense, buying a recreational property is a good long-term hold decision without doubt."

You can check out the possibility of recouping some of your costs by renting out your cottage or chalet, but the flip side is that it can be a hassle to constantly drive up to the property to clean up empty beer bottles and sweep the floor before the next renter arrives. However, there are now management companies that will book renters and look after the property for a portion of the rent. This is especially true of chalets at popular destinations. Management companies will book the renters, assume liability and scrub the bathtub after they have left. Usually the split on rent is about 50/50. With the property being used to generate income, you can pay down your recreational property sooner and get tax advantages as well.

No matter what, don't be an impulse buyer when buying any recreational property. Do comparative research to find out why a particular property is the best value or location for you. When you find a place that you want to buy or after you've short-listed a few properties, you should find a home inspector who is familiar with cottages who can look at it/them from every point of view. There are things that are unique to cottage properties that you might not have to consider in a metropolitan area, such as ant infestations eating away at the wood or whether you can drink the water. The last thing you want to do is buy a property where the well is just about to go dry. A home inspector familiar with cottage properties can give you an idea of what you can expect and warn you of any improvements that may be necessary.

taking steps toward effective home and tenant insurance

I consider home and tenant insurance as must-haves to protect you, your guests and your possessions. There are some steps you can take that will help you get the most out of them should you ever need to call on them.

Home Insurance

The best way to not be disappointed when it comes to making a claim on your home insurance is to know exactly what you've purchased. Make sure you have "guaranteed replacement cost" insurance on your home to ensure there will be enough money to rebuild it in case of catastrophic loss. If you have actual cash value coverage and your expensive plasma screen TV is stolen, you won't get a brand new one; depreciation will be taken into consideration and you will be given a cheque based on what it's worth now, not what you paid for it.

Just like car insurance claims have become something you should file only if you have a major event like an accident or your vehicle being stolen, the same is now true of home insurance. When you do make a claim, it should be a big one, because there is nothing that insurance companies hate more than claims. Claims can make your premiums rise and cause you to have your insurance canceled.

Finding savings with home insurance is difficult, but possible. One way to save money on your policy is to raise your deductible from $250 or $500 to $1,000. This can reduce your annual premiums by as much as 10% to 30%. Having a $1,000 deductible means you will have to come up with the first grand if you need to make a claim, but in 15 years of home ownership I never have and most of us don't. You can try combining home and auto insurance coverage for savings. Ask if there are deductions for fire extinguishers, a monitored burglar alarm and deadbolt locks. Generally speaking, if you are in a low claim zone your rates are low. If you're in a high claim zone, your rates are higher. It's best to review your coverage regularly and shop around to make sure you are getting the best rate possible.

Tenant Insurance

If you are a renter, you should have tenant insurance. Like mortgage insurance, it includes liability coverage and protects your possessions. This can protect you against unforeseen accidents that may damage another person or their property. It will protect you if someone slips in your apartment or if you damage other units in your building with an overflowing bathtub.

Home Inventory

If you did have a fire or were the victim of a break-in, could you remember everything you own? If your home burns down and you have $200,000 worth of contents coverage, you are not simply handed a cheque for $200,000. You will have to give a detailed list of everything that was lost. The fridge, dishwasher and big screen TV come to mind quickly, but jewellery, artwork, CD collections, pots and pans, curtains and all your clothing are difficult to remember.

Making an inventory is time consuming, but once it's done it's easy to update. A home video camera is a quick way to take inventory but an insurance company would rather see detailed lists, receipts and serial and model numbers. Once lists are made, they should be kept in a safe place, such as a safety deposit box or left with a friend or family member. Some insurance companies offer inventory lists to help you make an accurate record of your contents.

Additional Coverage

Special items, such as jewellery or hobby collections, should be appraised to give accurate assessments of their worth. They may require "a rider," which is additional insurance. Wedding rings, collectibles or expensive bikes may have a limited payout. For example, many policies will only pay $250 per bike unless you have purchased additional insurance.

You may be able to purchase coverage for exclusions, but even if not you should be aware of your policy's exclusions. Exclusions are certain things, such as "acts of God," that home insurance will generally not cover. A tree falling onto your house may not be covered. While a leaking hot water heater that floods your basement will be covered, a flood caused by water from *outside* your home will not be. Damage caused by ice dams (water freezing and backing up on your roof) and sewer backups are not necessarily covered unless you have ice dam and sewer backup coverage, which may be extra. Damage caused by a rotting roof, rodents or mudslides is also generally not covered.

You should never leave your home with an appliance running because this is often when fires and floods occur (like dryer fires due to unclean lint traps).

It's always a good idea when taking a vacation to shut off the main water valve that comes into your home, because most floods happen when people are away. Usually a hot-water hose on the back of the washing machine or a hose connected to the dishwasher bursts.

If you are planning to be away for more than four days, you may have to have someone check your home, or your insurance coverage could be voided. Check this important detail before taking a lengthy trip.

If you purchase a woodstove, buy a pool or add square footage to your home, you should notify your insurance company. You do not want to have something happen and then find out your coverage has limitations because you were not completely honest and forthcoming with your insurer. For many of us our home is our largest asset, so it's vital to make sure there is proper coverage in case of a major flood or fire.

renovating your home

If you plan to stay in a home for a long time, you may want to get your castle exactly as you want it, but always renovate with resale in mind. If your goal is to increase your sale price, you needn't spend tens of thousands of dollars remodeling kitchens, building home theatre rooms and putting in hot tubs. Some renovation projects will give you more bang for your buck when you sell your home.

> If you fix up your home a little at a time, you can enjoy the improvements. One project a year is easier to budget for than a major gutting of your home all at once.

Painting

The easiest and most inexpensive way to give a home a whole new look is to paint it from top to bottom. Before you do, you may want to have a colour consultant guide you. They will charge anywhere from $75 to $150 to come into your home, tell you the latest popular colours and trends and guide you on how you should paint the various rooms so your house "flows"—especially important in today's open concept homes. Colour consultants say they also act as marriage counsellors because often a colour chosen in a store doesn't look the same on the wall. Anyone who has had to repaint a room several times because a spouse didn't like the colour may find the services of a colour consultant worth it. I know I did. You can ask for them at most paint stores or look in the Yellow Pages under Interior Designers.

The Kitchen

The kitchen is now one of the most popular renovation areas for homeowners, and it's also one of the places where it's easy to go overboard and spend tens of thousands of dollars too much. A built-in refrigerator and professional-style range can cost $15,000; custom cabinets, another $40,000. Unless you are totally loaded with cash, there is no way you should be seriously considering spending this kind of money. You don't want to go on a $100,000 spending spree only to recoup 20% of your costs when you go to sell.

It really is possible to make responsible purchase decisions and end up with a beautiful, functional kitchen. You can get quality appliances at a fraction of the cost of professional-style ones and consumer research has shown that they are just as reliable. Paying more for fancy stoves, fridges and dishwashers doesn't always mean you won't have a breakdown. It's a good idea to upgrade the flooring and decor as well to give your hub a fresh look. Instead of getting new cupboards, you can replace old door handles and hinges with modern-looking hardware for a fresh appearance.

Bathrooms

Bathrooms are another place where the money you spend can be recouped at resale, especially in today's market where people want to turn their bathrooms into their own personal spa, a place to get away from a stress-filled day. Bathrooms are also places that show their age fast, so an update, even an inexpensive one, can help beautify your home and get it ready for resale. Again, you can go overboard in a washroom renovation and spend way too much. (I saw a $4,000 toilet in one high-end plumbing store.) Paint, tile, and new faucets and fixtures can be done relatively inexpensively. A soaker tub or new shower can add appeal or an old one can be refinished. If your home only has one or two bathrooms, consider adding another. An extra bathroom can help you avoid lineups now and pay off when you put your house up for sale later.

Fireplaces

A fireplace can be a pleasant addition for those cold winter nights, as people cocoon in their homes. It's also a renovation that can help you sell your home. A real wood-burning woodstove or fireplace can be a nice touch, but they're a lot of work and may cause your home insurance to increase. A better bet if you have natural gas in your home already is to get a gas-burning fireplace. They are pleasant to look at, help a house heat up quickly and you can turn them on and off with the flip of a switch. Electric fireplaces have also improved over the years and the new ones no longer have that cheesy look of an orange plastic flame over a heater fan. They are not too expensive, can heat a room within minutes and be set on a thermostat. They can even run without throwing heat for when you just want to set the mood. An electric fireplace can be a great addition to a home or condo and when you move you can take it with you.

Flooring

Good flooring can make all the difference. Nothing stands out more than old, damaged floors or stained and worn-out carpet. Hardwood floors are all the rage and can help add to the value of your home. If you're lucky, you may have some old hardwood floors under your wall-to-wall carpet, just waiting to be uncovered. Sanding and refinishing them can give a room a whole new look.

If hardwood is too expensive for your budget, laminate flooring looks almost as good at a fraction of the price. Carpeting or tile in neutral tones can also freshen up a home and give it a modern look.

Finished Basement

One of the best ways to add extra value to your home is to add square footage. While a new addition is a major renovation and huge project, refinishing a basement doesn't have to be. All of a sudden, a 2,000-square-foot home has another 1,000 square feet of living space. It's a great place to put a family room, pool table or home theatre. You'll be glad you made the investment and it will pay off when you put the house on the market.

Landscaping

Your home doesn't need to have the ultimate in landscape design, but it should at least be comparable to other homes in the neighbourhood. Curb appeal says a lot, especially when a potential buyer pulls up in front of your house. Low-maintenance hedges and trees, hanging baskets and a well-manicured lawn will help increase your home's appeal. A seating area in your backyard, possibly an interlock patio or a deck, will give you and a future homeowner a place to unwind in privacy.

Pools

Pools have become extremely popular and if you want one you will be faced with the same decision every pool owner must make: in-ground or above-ground? The in-ground pool is obviously the more appealing choice. However, in-ground pools are expensive—between $25,000 and $40,000. You will then have to pay for the landscaping around it.

While an in-ground pool is a beautiful addition to any home, an above-ground pool is too and may be the better choice. Why? They are a fraction of the price, at about $5,000. And they're practical, pleasing to look at and offer the same family fun as an in-ground pool.

In-ground pools limit your market when it comes time to sell your home since not everyone wants a pool. Some real estate studies have shown that the value of a home decreases as soon as a pool is put in. When buying a home with an in-ground pool, an agent will tell you you're getting the pool for free. When selling an above-ground pool, you can say to the person who wants to buy your home, "Do you want the pool or not? If you want it, you can have it. If you don't, I'll have it removed before you move in."

While pools are a lot of fun, they are also a lot of work—filters to clean, chemicals to add, pool openings and closings ... It may be worth it when your children are younger and enthusiastic about swimming, but once they're older the pool may lose some of its sparkle. I have seen neighbours whose children have left home who may use their pool only two or three times a summer. I've done stories where people have had to pay $10,000 to $15,000 to fill in a pool. Just weigh your options carefully before deciding and don't buy an in-ground just to "keep up with the Joneses."

dodging home renovation rip-offs

Every couple of weeks I get a call from a viewer with a complaint about home renovations. They always go the same way. "He seemed like a nice guy. He got right to work. He said he needed money up front to buy supplies. Once he got the money he never came back. When we phone him, we get a pager and he never calls us."

It's amazing how many people will research for months before buying a television set, but they entrust a complete stranger, just someone who left a flyer in their mailbox, with a $20,000 home renovation project. There are reputable, hard-working contractors out there, but unfortunately the profession is overrun with scam artists who start jobs with no intention of finishing them. Renovators may offer to save you money by doing a job "under the table" in order to avoid taxation, but not having the proper paper-work, contracts and receipts can lead to problems later. Even if a dishonest or unprofessional home renovator does complete the work, they will cut corners, use inferior materials and work shoddily. I have investigated cases where renovators have ripped off home-owners for hundreds to as much as $80,000.

Word of mouth is your best bet to find a good contractor because if a friend or family member has had a good experience with them, chances are you will, too. If you really can't find anyone on your own, check with the local building supply store to see if they can recommend someone reputable. Avoid contractors who come to your door or drop off flyers in your mailbox. And make sure you can get a hold of your contractor if you need to. When things are going well, your calls to a cell phone or pager will be returned, but when there is a problem they may disappear. Knowing their physical address can help, so you can track them down if things go wrong.

It's always a good idea to get at least three quotes on any major job. Work to be done should be detailed so it's not open to interpretation. If you want a toilet, you can pay $80 or $4,000 for one. If you don't make it clear which one you want, you will get the cheapest one on the market. One way to keep track of prices is to buy the items yourself, although a contractor may get a special rate on materials. For example, trees you would buy from a nursery may cost you $149, but contractors may get them for $79. You can use this information to negotiate an even better deal. If you buy the drywall and plumbing materials yourself, you will have them in your possession if a renovator quits before the project is complete. You can also write a cheque directly to a building supplies store and have the materials delivered straight to your home.

Another good idea is to never pay too much money up front. A contractor may say they need a 30% deposit to secure them and then another 30% to begin. This means you have given them half the money before they've done anything! If you're going to get lousy work, that's when it will begin and when you complain they just won't come back. If a contractor is too eager to get money before starting a job, this may be a clear sign they're not legitimate. Even a reputable contractor may require some money up front to buy materials, but the amount should not be excessive.

One major problem with renovations occurs when people don't have a clear plan set out for their renovations. There should be a contract that spells out the details.

- How much will labour cost?
- How much will materials cost?
- Is the contractor responsible for the debris left behind? Will they transport it to the dump or will you?
- What is the warranty or guarantee?
- Is the quote a firm price or could it change halfway through the project?

All your plans and instructions should be put in writing because verbal promises mean nothing when a problem arises.

Most bad renovators are knowledgeable as to how the law works, so when you say you will call the police they don't care. If a renovator takes $35,000 from you and does absolutely no work, it's fraud; however, if they begin the job and then quit, it's a civil matter for the courts. The police won't get involved, you may need a lawyer and even if you win your case you're still not assured of getting your money back. That's why it's so important to choose the right contractor.

> Is there a way to know for sure how much experience a contractor has so you can be sure you are getting a quality job? Do they have similar projects that you can see and references that you can check?

selling your home

Properly preparing your home for sale can increase its value dramatically. Making the right moves could help you profit tens of thousands of dollars.

A new tactic being used by some real estate agents is house staging. They will hire a "staging team" to come into your home and make cosmetic changes to make it feel like an upscale property. According to Dianne Usher, area manager with Royal LePage and director of The Canadian Real Estate Association, "House staging and preparing your home for sale is not a new phenomenon, but we've put it into a different package and we are promoting it now whereas we weren't before." Stagers may repaint rooms, rent upscale furniture, hang expensive paintings and bring in art sculptures. They will even go to the trouble of adding a grand piano if it can create a certain ambience in a home that could add thousands to its asking price.

You can pay a stager $250 for advice and an hour or two of their time to come to your home and make suggestions, or you can pay them thousands to paint the walls, redecorate and hang expensive art.

In the red-hot Toronto real estate market it may be worth spending $20,000 on house staging to try to add another $50,000 to your selling price. That being said, if you are selling a house in a rural area or small town, even the most expensive Picasso may not be enough to have someone buy your home—there has to be a reason to move there.

Renting furniture to help you sell your house might seem extreme but Usher says, "The quicker a home sells the more money you can make." I know myself from touring large, empty homes how impersonal and cold they can feel. It's why model homes look so great—they are loaded with the latest interior design trends and modern furniture.

Usher is adamant that staging is not just for high-end homes. "Even if you are selling a modest home, if you have unfurnished rooms you can rent sofas for the living room, a dining room table and art for the walls. Homes can be empty because of a marital situation or because the house is brand new."

Timothy Badgley is an interior designer and owner of Acanthus Interiors in Port Hope, Ontario, who says many homes are in need of a pre-sale makeover. "The good news is that unlike major renovations, house staging is a simple and inexpensive way to bring your home up to date." He suggests 10 things you can do before putting your house up for sale.

1. Keep It Clean

Is every room neat, spotlessly clean, dusted and uncluttered? Steam clean carpets and wax floors. Wash walls, heating and A/C vents and light fixtures. Pay special attention to bathrooms and the kitchen. Make sure tile grout is mildew free and baseboards are scrubbed. Clean the refrigerator and stove, as well as the washer and dryer. Don't forget about windows! Make sure that all windowpanes, ledges and blinds are spic and span. Ensure taps are drip free, drains flow and toilets don't run and run.

2. Lose the Clutter

Have a yard sale or take old furniture, clothing and knick-knacks to Goodwill. Organize shelves, put away items and purge your home of unnecessary items. Make sure that your kitchen and bathroom counters are free of small appliances and personal effects. Some businesses will come and pick up your junk for free.

3. Create the Illusion of Space

After decluttering, reorganize. Remove excess furniture to make rooms feel more open. An oversized couch can actually make a room seem smaller than it is, so consider moving it out and replacing it with a smaller couch, or if it's a sectional, remove one of the sections. Clean and organize your closets. Store unnecessary items somewhere else or rent a temporary storage unit. Use strategically placed mirrors to create the illusion of more space.

4. De-personalize Your Home

Make your home "anonymous" so that buyers can envision it as their potential home. Put away any family photos, sports trophies, collectibles, knick-knacks and souvenirs. This will also help to remove clutter and create more space.

5. Freshen It Up

Adding a fresh coat of paint and laying new carpet will clean and brighten up your home. Choose neutral colours and make them consistent throughout the home. If you choose to wallpaper, make sure that the paper is properly applied, your colour choice is neutral and patterns are kept to a minimum.

6. Make a Good First Impression

Walking into a home with fingerprinted screen door windows or cluttered entranceways can influence a potential homebuyer's decision. Strong odours can ruin a sale, so pay attention to pet, cooking and cigarette smells. Light delicately scented candles or have cookies baking in the oven when you're showing. Fresh flowers can help to brighten and energize your home.

7. Enhance Curb Appeal

Homebuyers decide whether or not to look inside a house by the appearance of your home's exterior. Paint or wash the outside of your home. Keep your lawn trimmed and flowerbeds weeded. Clear the driveway and yard of children's toys and unsightly trash cans. Use urns to define walkways and ensure that windows are clean. Replace broken or dated light fixtures. If you have a garage, make certain it's neat and clutter free.

8. Make Modern Choices

Ensure that the decor of your home is modern and tasteful. Replace outdated furniture, wall coverings and window treatments. Add colour to the neutral tones on your walls and floors with removable items such as throw pillows or bedding. To create a minimalist and contemporary space, steer away from too many personal touches.

9. Relocate the Pets

Take your pets with you when your house is being shown, or at least keep them outside. Pets under foot will quickly put a damper on an otherwise positive showing. Make sure your house is odour free and spotless. Be sure to empty and hide unsightly kitty litter, lint brush your furniture and put your furry friend's toys, dishes and scratching post away during showings.

10. Beautify Your Backyard

A house showing doesn't end at the back door—buyers will be influenced by the state of your backyard. Keep the lawn, hedges and flowerbeds manicured. Try to recreate an entertaining area by cleaning, sweeping decks, and setting up patio furniture. Put away gardening tools and kids' toys. If you have a pool, ensure that the cover is pulled back, the water is inviting, the lining is algae free and pool supplies are stored. Buyers may want to look in your garden shed, so keep it organized and clean.

Even if you're not putting your house up for sale, it's a good idea to have it appraised every year or two just to see what it's worth on the market. While the bank will do this for a fee, you can have a real estate agent do it for free. They, of course, will hope that you will use them when you go to sell and if you are satisfied with their services you just might.

It can also be a good boost to know that as you pay down your home it's also increasing in value. Of course, it's not as gratifying if you find out your home has gone down in value. It will all depend on the current market conditions.

For more information on house staging, check out www.totaltransformations.net.

CHAPTER 54

earning money at home

Many of us would love the opportunity to make cash from home, either as a full-time or part-time job. Whether you're a stay-at-home parent, student, retiree, someone who wants part-time income while looking for full-time work, or someone who wants to work full-time from the comfort of your own home, it can be beneficial to earn income while staying home. Unfortunately, this is an area where many shameless scam artists rip off people.

> We've all seen the ads saying you can get rich stuffing envelopes, assembling products or reviewing books. While most of these job opportunities are scams, you should not be deterred because it is possible to earn money working from home.

Belinda Hansen is the founder of www.canadianhomeworker.com and a long-time home worker. In 1997, she put a career in the media on hold to take care of her children and her father, who had suffered a stroke. Knowing she would be at home for an indefinite period, she began to search out legitimate jobs for the home worker. "A lot of people think it's just stay-at-home moms who want to work from home. While they are a large group of the stay-at-home workers, there are also people not satisfied with their regular workplace, from

CEOs to managers on down. They may feel stuck in a rut and want to explore and try something new and exciting," says Hansen.

I get complaints from people who paid to sign up for jobs stuffing envelopes and, of course, the job never materialized (machines stuff envelopes at the rate of thousands per hour, so this isn't a realistic job for people to do efficiently). Another popular scam is jewellery assembly—you pay in advance for a kit that comes in the mail. Hansen says, "You actually get a kit with pieces of jewellery, beads and wires, and they ask you to create the jewellery according to their instructions. You send the completed jewellery back and they send you a note saying your work was not up to their standards of quality control. They then have your money and the jewellery, which they sell, and of course you get nothing." Another popular scam gets you buying a book that promises a listing of companies that hire home workers. The books are usually $50 and if they do send you one at all, it's filled with outdated, useless information.

The key to not getting pulled into a scam is to never spend money in advance to get the job. "If someone is asking you for money in order to work at home, that is definitely the number one red flag that a job is not legitimate. Another red flag is if you are asked to work ahead of time without a contract."

So what kind of work can you do from home? Running a daycare, offering music lessons, baking, tutoring, cutting hair, tele-marketing, pet sitting, sewing, data entry, fundraising, Internet translation and customer service are just a few of the jobs available.

You should try something that you truly like and are interested in, possibly turning a hobby into a money-making venture. Hansen says, "I always tell people to look inside of themselves and think about what they would really like to do. Do they have a certain skill set that they have always wanted to pursue or make into a full-time career? You can't do something successfully from home unless you actually love it." To be successful you will have to be persistent. "You need to think about ... how many hours [you] can

… put in to do that job. If you can only do it five hours a day, don't take on a job that will involve so much work it will be keeping you up at night."

I did a story with a woman who thought that brides should have the option to rent their wedding dress instead of buying it. She created a business whereby she buys wedding dresses from women who just got married and then rents the gowns to new brides. It's turned into a very successful business and it's run out of her home. (You can check out the company's website at www.gowngoround.com.)

Hansen agrees that sometimes the best job you can get is one you invent for yourself; but if that's not possible, Hansen claims, "The best thing you can do is network. I always encourage people to go to their local chamber of commerce and try to join a business group. There may even be a woman's business networking club. Your local chamber of commerce can help provide you with all kinds of contacts who may be able to use your services." If you're a great writer or have desktop computer skills, someone may need that kind of help in the community. Find out if there is a need for a fashion designer, cook or seamstress. Businesses may need home workers to input data into websites or call customers. Companies also hire people for work overflow in case a secretary or researcher needs help catching up. In time, you could be able to develop your talent into a stand-alone business.

There are also tax advantages to working at home. Hansen says, "You could work at a job and earn $80,000 annually but only take home about half that … When you work from home, you could actually make $40,000 working on contract. You add GST if you have a GST number and you're actually making more than when you were earning an $80,000 salary." I'll have more on home business taxes shortly.

What you don't get working at home are job benefits. "What works best is if one person can work at home and have a spouse that works for a company that has benefits. Therefore, one has the flexibility to work their own hours and look after the family while the other has the base of security with benefits to help make the family secure." That's not possible for everyone but it may work for many people.

There are also job auction sites, such as Elance at www.elance.com. At this site, projects are put up for bid and you basically bid against other people to get the job. Hansen says, "It's for freelancers, Web designers, writers, researchers and graphic artists." The only problem is that bidders get into a frenzy and drive the price down, and the lowest bid always seems to win. The site is not for everyone but may be worth checking out depending on your skills.

As for Hansen, she says her current employer liked her so much they developed a full-time job around her skills and timetable. "My job has turned into many things. I'm so used to working at home now I will bake a cake or dinner, and then come back to my computer and work, and then go back to doing something else. I have people working for me now and it seems strange because those people are at the office and I am managing them from home. I'm also really glad I can be here for my family, and for me that's just the most important thing." For more information, advice and tips on working from home, check out Hansen's website at www.canadianhomeworker.com.

Tax Advantages of a Home Business

If you decide to work from home there are excellent tax advantages that can help make a home business extremely profitable. Evelyn Jacks is one of Canada's top tax advisors and is also the author of bestseller *Make Sure It's Deductible*. In the book, she discusses how to start a tax-efficient small business, write off deductions, make smart asset purchases, benefit from your home office and auto and put your family on the payroll and write them off.

Jacks says, "In order to get the tax advantages, what you have to be is diligent with your record keeping and you have to think of tax first in every expenditure that you are considering making." To do this, open a separate business bank account and have a separate credit card for business expenses. This helps with your record keeping because you're keeping your business and regular expenses separate. Jacks says, "It also preserves all your personal affairs for your tax auditors, as you should never give a tax auditor a reason to go through all your personal and business affairs."

One of the most lucrative tax deductions for any home business is the ability to write off a portion of your home as a home office. It must be a separate space away from the rest of the living area of the home and you can prorate your home expenditures according to square footage of that separate office space. These write-offs include mortgage interest, property taxes, maintenance, utilities, etc. The home office could be 10% to 20% of your home depending on the size of your business and can lead to major deductions.

If you have a home business that requires you to use a car, you will need to have an automobile expense log to show the total distance driven every year and how much of it's for business and personal use. You really should keep good driving records, as Jacks says, "This is one of the most audited areas on the tax return and most people really have trouble keeping that log. Due diligence is important because small business owners have a greater risk of an audit than someone who is filing just one T4 slip, a copy of which the employer sends directly to Canada's Revenue Agency."

Expenditures fall into two categories. First there are those that are used up in the normal case of business, like wages and office supplies, and are 100% deductible. The second group is capital expenditures, assets that depreciate over time. Jacks says many people make mistakes there. "For example, they put a new roof on their garage for a business and they want to write that off completely on their taxes. That improves the useful life of the asset so it must be written off over time," says Jacks. There are certain restricted expenditures; things like meals have a 50% restriction.

Having all your business affairs in order will do you no good if what you're operating is not a real business. It's only legitimate if you can show a reasonable expectation of profit. I remember a story about a magician in rural Newfoundland who ran his business at a loss for 17 years. Finally the federal government told him he could not make a living as a magician in rural Newfoundland and denied his claim. This may have been a case of someone pulling a rabbit out of a hat a few times a year to write off expenses and claiming he had a legitimate small business (but it did work for 17 years!). Jacks says, "If you have a hobby that has no expectation of profit, the government is not going to allow you to write off your losses." Jacks says recently the government has firmed up requirements and proposed that you need to show profit not just year-over-year but also on a cumulative basis over the life of the business.

It's quite common for businesses to have to spend money in order to make it, so spending $10,000 today to acquire a contract that could help translate into $20,000 worth of income is acceptable because there is clearly a reasonable expectation of profit. If year-over-year, either because of mismanagement or lack of revenue from your activities, you continually write-off losses, then the government will say this does not show legitimacy as a business enterprise. You must show a reasonable expectation of profit within a reasonable time frame. Jacks says, "It boils down to simple business planning, because why would you spend time and money on an activity unless there was a reasonable expectation of profit for you? Most people in business don't intentionally go out to lose money. If it is your intention to build your endeavour into a profitable enterprise, then absolutely you can write off car expenses, a home office, the cost of assistance, advertising and many other things."

The act governing taxation is not specific about what you can and cannot write off; it just gives guidance. You have to think about each individual item you want to buy. Is it an expenditure incurred to earn income? If the answer is yes, then it's deductible. You can hire family members, but you have to show that they have worked for you in a job that you would have hired a stranger to do and at similar wages. Jacks says, "Don't just try to pay people a lump sum at the end of the year. You should be able to show the person was on the payroll and that proper record keeping took place. I find that many family businesses miss out on legitimate deductions that could have helped them earn extra income."

More deductions equal a larger refund, which can be used to help pay down debt or finance future projects for your business. For more information, check out Jacks' website at www.knowledgebureau.com.

thinking seriously about cars

For most of us, after our home, the next largest purchase we will make is our vehicle. I want to dedicate several chapters to owning and operating a car because it's an area where many people waste money—simply getting from A to B!

I get the urge to buy a brand new high-end luxury car as much as the next person. You are what you drive right? That's the message car companies would have us believe. Now, there is nothing wrong with driving an expensive car if you can afford it. However, when it comes to cars too many people are trying to keep up with the Joneses! They are spending thousands of dollars a year more than they need to, trying to maintain an image that is unrealistic for their bank balance.

Someone once told me they got a great deal on a car. "What was it?" I asked. They said they had purchased a luxury import that was listed at $72,000 but they got it for only $65,000. In their mind this was an incredible savings—a steal of a deal. The only thing I could see was that he paid $65,000 for a car that couldn't hold a set of golf clubs.

The price of a car is just the start. There are many other costs associated with luxury car ownership.

- What kind of gas will this luxury car take? High octane, no doubt. Add another 10 cents a litre to every litre of gas you will pump into this car for as long as you own it.

- How much is car insurance? Higher for sure, and many people don't even bother to check this before they sign a contract to buy a new car.

- This beautiful new set of wheels may be a target for thieves. Do you have a security system for the car? You'll need one.

- How much is regular maintenance? Is an oil change going to be $75 instead of $30?

- Is special maintenance required because it is a fancy import?

- Is the hourly rate for mechanics $20 an hour more because it's a luxury car?

- What about parts? Will they be harder to find and cost you more because the car is not a mass-produced domestic car?

Don't get me wrong. There is nothing wrong with luxury car ownership if you can afford it. If your house is paid for, the kids are done university and your credit line is paid off and you must have a luxury vehicle to reward yourself, then go ahead. Just realize there are added costs to buying a luxury car or even a brand new car for that matter. In the following chapters we will look at ways to drive dependable cars at reasonable prices, which will get you where you have to go and still allow you to save money and pay down debt.

buying a
new car

If you have attained a certain level of wealth and feel you must have a brand new car, then you will want to make sure that you get the best deal you can. (Still, I would strongly advise you to read chapter 59 on buying *nearly new*, because I feel that nearly new is one of the best values in the car marketplace today.)

> If you are deep in debt, a new car is the last thing you should be buying. I asked Dennis DesRosiers, one of Canada's leading independent automotive consultants, what someone in debt should buy and he said, "If you are buried in debt, stick with the car that you have. Don't go into additional debt to buy a vehicle. A new car is one of the worst debts that you can possibly add to your ledger. If you have a high debt load and you are desperate for a vehicle, buy a beater. It's amazing how high the quality is of nine- and 10-year-old used cars in the marketplace."

If you feel you must have a new car, be ready to deal when stepping into a showroom. DesRosiers says, "It is shocking how many consumers walk into a dealership and have zero understanding on what kind of vehicle they want or the way they plan to pay for it. The worst three words you can tell a dealer are 'I don't know.' You really have to do your homework and be prepared."

There are three elements to any good negotiating process: time, information and money.

Time. If you have time on your side and don't need a vehicle right away, you can shop around, compare the competition and wait for a sale or financing offer. If you don't, and need a car right away, you may get stuck having to buy something that's not really what you want and pay too much money.

Information. With the Internet, new car reviews, manufacturers' websites and independent publications, there is a wealth of information on vehicle pricing, fuel economy, reliability, options, comfort, space and performance. A good buyer can walk into a showroom knowing as much or more about a car than the salesperson selling it.

Money. Before you go to buy a car you should know how you are going to pay for it. You should be pre-approved at your bank or at least have a good idea about the vehicle financing that will be offered. Too many people choose a car without thinking clearly about how they will pay for it.

As for new car pricing, something interesting has been happening in the marketplace. DesRosiers says, "From a pure MSRP (manufacturers' suggest retail price) point of view, the average price of vehicles has deflated. It has gone down on [the] equivalent product for five years in a row in Canada. The fact that the MSRP has been going down has led consumers and the industry to option these vehicles up and to sell higher trim levels, so the average price of a vehicle is actually increasing. Buyers are getting a lot more options and accessories." So while list prices drop, real prices go up. That's why when you see a car selling for $19,999, it costs about $35,000 when you drive away in it.

It's not just the options that add to the price, however—it is the taxes and fees to get a new car out the door. The average new car transaction price in the industry is about 22% above MSRP. DesRosiers says the new vehicle is the largest tax target in this country, and it's true. You have to add federal and provincial sales taxes, tire tax, air conditioning tax, energy taxes and environmental taxes, dealer preparation, delivery charges, etc.

And once you pay all these fees and taxes, the car drops in price dramatically as soon as you drive it off the lot! DesRosiers explains, "It depends on the brand, but generally speaking, a new car depreciates 20% to 30% the day you drive it off the car dealer's lot." That means if you buy a new car, you are paying all the taxes and charges just to get it on the road. Do you think the person who buys it after you will thank you for that? I doubt it.

If you are buying a new car you have to consider what it may be worth when you go to sell it. DesRosiers says, "The average price of a four-year-old Honda passenger car last year was somewhere between 50% and 60% of its original MSRP. The average resale price of a GM, Ford or Chrysler was somewhere between 30% and 40% of its original MSRP. A consumer who bought a Honda for $37,000 could still sell it four years later for $25,000. The consumer who may have thought he got a great deal buying a new GM at $32,000—$5,000 less—may find when he goes to sell it in four years [that] it's only worth $12,000." So when you are buying new, you're better off to purchase a high resale value vehicle, which will be worth more when you go to sell it or trade it in.

> The average new car transaction price in the industry is about 22% above MSRP.

If you must buy new, be aware that new car models are coming out earlier and earlier. I had one couple call me who were upset that they bought a 2005 Volkswagen in the spring of 2005 only to see a new 2006 model parked beside it when they went to pick it up.

They hadn't even driven their new car off the lot and it was already one model year old.

DesRosiers says typically dealers clear out models in the August to November time frame and may offer discounts, but by buying late in the model year the vehicle will lose one year of depreciation very quickly. This isn't a big issue if you plan to keep it for seven or eight years, but it is if you plan to trade it in in a year or two, because the resale value will be lower.

Take the vehicle for a test drive and DesRosiers recommends that you test-drive the dealership as well to ensure they are trustworthy, professional and knowledgeable. DesRosiers says, "I believe consumers should trust their gut. If deep down they feel uncomfortable with a dealership, then they should go somewhere else."

Before deciding on any car, call your insurance company to see how much it will cost for insurance. Premiums vary widely depending on the make and model. A luxury or sports car can have substantially higher premiums than a family sedan.

There are a few last-minute but important details to consider. Don't rush the financing; the buyer who shops first and worries about financing later could be in for an unpleasant surprise. Watch out for extras when closing the deal, such as rustproofing, undercoating and other dealer options that may be done elsewhere at a cheaper price. If you are trading in a vehicle, know what it's worth and consider selling it privately to get more money for it. Again consider if you really need a brand new car. If you are planning to keep it for a long time and can afford it, go ahead. If you are trying to pay off debt, consider the nearly new car—it's really the better option.

financing
at 0%

Financing at 0%! Wow, let's all buy a new car! There are few offers as enticing when looking for a new set of wheels as 0% financing. When you do the straight calculations comparing an interest rate of 0% to 7$\frac{1}{2}$% on a $20,000 car loan over 24 months it shows you can save $1,600. Over 36 months you can save almost $2,400. On a $35,000 car loan over three years you can keep an extra $4,200 in your pocket. Sounds great! I'll take a new car for me and my wife! Zero percent financing is a no-brainer, right? Well, think again. The problem is in the fine print, which reveals zero percent offers don't equal zero percent at all.

There are drawbacks to these loans. Often they are used to get you in the door along with other offers like "zero down" and "zero payments for six months." Car dealers aren't in the charity business and most of these offers are designed to get money from you one way or another. An incentive up front usually means higher costs down the road. It's up to you to calculate which approach is best for you.

The advertising for 0% financing is very misleading. If you read the fine print you'll see that taking a loan with the dealer at 0% means you'll have to "forgo certain cash incentives." Well, those cash incentives really add up. You may find you are far better off borrowing the money from your bank and paying cash for the car rather than going for any 0% financing deal. Check out the fine print in this 0% financing ad from a major manufacturer having a sale on new cars and trucks:

> "If customers choose 0% financing, they forgo additional incentives available to cash purchasers. The effective interest rate factoring in these incentives could be up to 8.5%."

What? They're admitting that 0% financing is really the equivalent of an 8.5% interest rate? Yep. There has been pressure on auto manufacturers to make financing details clearer for consumers. They're doing so, but often the clearer details are buried in the fine print. Not every 0% deal will be equal to 8.5% because the cash incentives will vary, but it's clear that 0% financing is not really as it seems.

If a rebate is offered, your best deal may be to take the rebate and borrow money from your bank. If the rebate being offered is $3,000, let's see how that compares to 0% financing.

	0% Financing	Bank Loan
Price of the vehicle	$20,000	$20,000
Rebates or cash incentives	–	$3,000
Amount financed	$20,000	$17,000
Number of months in loan term	36	36
Loan interest rate	–	7%
Monthly payment	$555.56	$524.91

With the 0% financing offer, your payment would actually be $30.65 higher every month. Over the life of the three-year loan, you would actually pay $1,103.40 more for the car. So much for 0% financing on this deal!

Even if you were to take this same car loan over four years you would still be better off with the bank loan at 7%.

	0% Financing	Bank Loan
Price of the Vehicle	$20,000	$20,000
Rebates or Cash Incentives	–	$3000
Amount Financed	$20,000	$17,000
Number of Months in Loan Term	48	48
Loan Interest Rate	–	7%
Monthly Payment	$416.67	$407.09

With 0% financing you would still pay $459.84 more than if you took out a loan at the bank at 7%!

When you are buying a car there may not be a rebate offer, but if you are paying cash there is usually a "cash price" that can be several thousand dollars cheaper than the list price. A shrewd negotiator can save hundreds or even thousands of dollars off the list price. As soon as a dealer knows you are interested in the 0% financing offer, they will usually bring all negotiating to a standstill. They will assume you don't have the money to pay cash for the car and take away your bargaining power. "Sorry. Can't go any lower—not with 0% financing. I'm already losing my shirt on this deal." That's not true. The price of the car and the cost of financing are two separate issues. Also, keep in mind that ...

- You may need a perfect credit rating to qualify for 0% financing.
- There may be a shorter loan period, larger monthly payments and the offer may only be good on a limited number of models or cars left in the showroom (ones the dealer is trying to get rid of).
- Offers of 0% financing can also be used as a "bait and switch" tactic. You are lured into the showroom with promises of 0% financing only to find out you don't qualify. Of course, then

the dealer shows you other cars that he can sell you "with financing to fit your budget."

Now, all of this doesn't mean you should ignore 0% offers, but you should run calculations before signing any contract. You can find calculators online that can help you determine which is the better deal for you by typing "zero percent financing vs. rebates" in any search engine. I found a good calculator at www.consumerreports.org. Keep in mind that you're better off with a good used car anyway, which I'll address soon, in chapters 59 and 60.

leasing a vehicle

So you want to lease a vehicle. Why? Do you really want to rent a car instead of own it? Do you really want to pay hundreds of dollars a month for years and then give the car back to a dealer so he can sell it for a profit? Do you really want to pay for wear and tear, scratches and dents and excess kilometres before giving the car to someone else? When you lease a car your name is not on the ownership, the leasing company's name is. Leasing is just a long-term rental.

As you have probably guessed, I believe leasing is a bad choice for most people. Years ago when I pressured a dealer on the true costs of leasing, he broke down and admitted that leasing is the most expensive way to get into a new car.

There are those who say rent what depreciates and own what appreciates, but this is not the case when it comes to a car. If you can't afford to buy it, you can't afford to lease it. Ralph Nader, consumer advocate and presidential candidate, warned American consumers years ago when leasing was first introduced that it was more like "auto fleecing than leasing." Phil Edmonston, author of the popular series of Lemon-Aid Used Car Guides, says, "Leasing a new or used vehicle is almost never a good idea unless you can put the capital you will save to work in your own enterprise and get much more money out of it for your endeavours." He continues, "If you can't afford a vehicle and must lease one in order to afford it, then you should go immediately to the used car choices. Overall, leasing is a means whereby sellers give you the illusion that an over-priced new vehicle is a reasonable buy."

Why do people lease? A lower monthly payment is the main reason. Driving a vehicle that is covered under warranty is another. For many people it's also a chance to "upsize" the car they drive (they may really only be able to afford a minivan, but through leasing they can have a luxury SUV for the same monthly payment). There may also be a "down payment" required at the beginning of a lease that does not build up equity in the vehicle; it's just a leasing payment in advance to make the monthly payments seem smaller.

When you add up the monthly payments, down payment, interest rates, additional fees and taxes, leasing starts to look like a profit generator for car companies. It is, which is why dealers spend a lot of money advertising and advocating leasing as a low-cost alternative to get into a new car. Many car companies now make more money off the financing of vehicles than they do on the cars themselves.

Don't believe the hype—leasing is *not* all that great. When you lease a vehicle you never build up equity in it the same way as if you were making loan payments (remember, it's really a rental). There are also added costs to leasing that are spelled out in the fine print (that no one ever bothers to read). And there are limitations to what you can do with the car, because you don't own it! Here are some things to think about.

Repairs

You may have to repair minor scratches and dents. And larger damages, which you'd get fixed when you had the money, may have to be done immediately. One viewer told me that two months before she was to turn in her car she bumped into a light pole in her parking lot. She didn't want to tell her insurance company because she didn't want a claim to raise her premiums. She had to spend $2,500 of her own money to repair the car before handing it over to the leasing company. If it was her own car she could have waited to repair the dent (or even left it as is, if she wanted) but couldn't because it was a lease.

Also, keep in mind that when you lease a car you have to pay for the oil changes and general maintenance. Any major non-accident-related repairs should be (but are not always) covered under warranty.

Excessive Wear and Tear

You could be charged for excessive wear and tear and if you miscalculate the number of kilometres you planned to drive you could be hit with hundreds or even thousands of dollars in excess kilometre charges. A lease may allow someone to drive 20,000 kilometres annually for a total of 60,000 kilometres over three years, but if a consumer racks up 76,000 kilometres during the lease contract they will be hit with an excess kilometre penalty charge. If the charge is $0.13 for every kilometre over the limit, that 16,000 excess kilometres would mean an additional charge of $2,080!

A cigarette burn in the carpet or a rip in the seat also allows the leasing company to charge you for excess wear and tear. They could even charge you for balding or mismatched tires. The excess wear and tear clause is one area where a dishonest dealer can try to line his pockets, getting you to pay for minor problems. Your security deposit may help if you left one, but make sure you get your security deposit back if there is nothing wrong with the car.

Travel Limitations

Because your name is not on the ownership, some leasing deals forbid you from removing the vehicle from your province or territory for an extended period unless you have permission from the leasing company. It's kind of like needing Mom or Dad's approval to take the car somewhere. (Who needs to relive that!)

A Lease Is a Binding Agreement

Another problem arises when people sign long-term leases and die, lose their job, get divorced or experience a major life change. Sure that two-seater sports car was great when you were single, but it won't be so handy with a baby on the way. I have done stories where a husband has leased an expensive pickup truck and then dies, leaving the leased truck to a widow who doesn't even drive. Still, she is expected to make the payments.

Many people believe incorrectly that they can simply hand the vehicle back over to a car dealership if all of a sudden they don't need it. But you have signed a contract and the dealer will expect you to fulfill your end of the bargain.

Types of Leases

You also have to be very careful what kind of lease you sign. In a closed lease, the most common kind used by major dealerships, you make a set number of payments during a specific time period of (usually) two, three or four years. In an open-end lease, you also make a set number of payments over a specific time frame, but here's where this kind of lease differs: when you bring the vehicle back, you may have to make one last payment to cover the difference between "the actual value of the vehicle" and its "residual value." This means the car dealer could hit you for an additional payment of hundreds or even thousands of dollars. For example, if the vehicle had a residual value of $12,000 but the leasing company could sell it for only $10,000 you would have to pay an additional fee of $2,000. If the vehicle is sold for more than the residual value, the consumer *might* be refunded the difference—*like that would ever happen!*

If you can't afford to buy it, you can't afford to lease it.

At the time of writing this, I have just been contacted by a young couple who signed an open-ended lease. They turned the car into the dealer, who sold it for $8,500 and then ordered them to make an additional payment of $2,200. Needless to say, they were shocked! They had not read the contract and were upset that the money they had been saving to buy a new car would now have to be used to make one final payment on a car they would never own.

If you do have to get out of a lease midway through your contract, you may have to try to sublease the vehicle to someone else (www.leasebusters.com is a website that for a fee brings together people who are looking to get into and out of car leases). You may have to purchase the car at a buyout price set by the leasing company or make the monthly payments until you have fulfilled your obligation. Either way, you could be on the hook for thousands of dollars to get out of a leasing deal.

Lease Length

Avoid leases longer than the manufacturer's warranty. Some dealers may try to get you to sign a 39-month lease rather than 36 to make the payments seem lower. However, when the warranty is up, you could be required to make repairs to the vehicle prior to giving it back.

Don't lease after December 31st, as you will then be leasing a car model that's half year old. Cars depreciate quickly, so if you must lease, strike a deal when the new models come out, which is usually between September and December. You can also shop deals around to see if the car you want to lease can be found cheaper somewhere else.

I realize that some consumers feel that leasing is for them. Some drivers who lease say they don't mind the perpetual monthly payment as long as it allows them to drive a new car that is under warranty. If you must have a new car every three years, take excellent care of vehicles, drive less than the annual mileage allowed in a leasing agreement and hate haggling with car dealers over trade-ins, then maybe leasing is for you *if* you realize this is the most expensive way to drive a new car.

Do the math on purchasing a two- or three-year-old car instead of leasing a new one and you may find that you will pay less in loan interest than leasing finance charges and you could have a similar monthly payment. You will also end up *owning* the car and not *renting* it.

CHAPTER 59

buying a used car
—"nearly new"

I continue to believe the best value on the road today is the "nearly new" vehicle, which is a vehicle up to four years old. As many consumers lease new cars and are forced by their contracts to take good care of them, every year there are hundreds of thousands of nearly new cars put up for sale. Leasing accounts for about 40% of new car purchases, and since consumers can walk away at the end of their lease, many do. The last five vehicles I have purchased have been two- to four-year-old vehicles that have just come off of a lease.

Canada's leading automotive expert, Dennis DesRosiers, says a new car depreciates about 20% to 30% as soon as it is driven off the lot, so if you buy that same vehicle a year or two later, you can save a lot of money.

On average, vehicles depreciate about 10% a year after their initial depreciation, but how much really depends on the manufacturer. DesRosiers says, "The brands that play heavily into the fleet markets—the ones that sell a lot to daily rentals, government agencies and utilities—have their vehicles depreciate quicker than the companies that don't sell into fleets." That's why GM, Ford and Chrysler typically have lower resale values on many of their products and Toyota and Honda tend to have higher resale values. It's why one- to four-year-old domestic vehicles can be an excellent value. GM, Ford and Chrysler products can be a tremendous deal because of their huge depreciation.

While a few years ago you could buy a two-year-old domestic vehicle with about 80,000 kilometres on it for half of its original selling price, this has changed slightly. Phil Edmonston of the Lemon-Aid series of car guides says, "It used to be two to three years old was the best deal on a nearly new car. It's really been moving to almost three or four years old because the depreciation really becomes important in about the third or fourth year." I noticed this myself with the last car that I bought. After buying two-year-old domestic cars that were half their price, I had to buy a car that was three years old to get the best value possible.

Edmonston says part of the reason for the shift is "because of the resurgence of the used car buyer in the market and people realizing the terrific value of used cars." Nearly new vehicles may still have some of the manufacturer's warranty remaining, and because of their age have the latest designs and safety features. While used vehicle sales used to average 1.4 million units annually a decade ago, Canadians are now buying 2.2 to 2.4 million used cars every year.

While you may have shied away from used cars in the past, the nearly new car is not someone else's problem. Nowadays a vehicle should last up to 300,000 kilometres, whereas 20 years ago they lasted only 150,000 kilometres. DesRosiers says, "New vehicles are of such high quality you can't help but end up with high-quality used cars. The invasion of high-quality Japanese vehicles forced everybody up the learning curve. So over the last decade it is unusual to have a low-quality vehicle manufactured. Just about every vehicle is currently well manufactured and that has resulted in an incredibly high-value used vehicle marketplace."

One of the best ways to get a deal on a vehicle is to find one that has just come off a lease. You can find these off-lease cars privately or on a dealer lot. DesRosiers has an excellent formula to help you calculate the value of a nearly new car. The average vehicle lasts about 300,000 kilometres and costs about $30,000; the capital cost to own a new vehicle is about $0.10 per kilometre over its lifetime. This calculation can be used to determine the value of a nearly new vehicle as well. Divide the price by 300,000 kilometres minus the odometer reading.

A three-year-old vehicle selling for $25,000 with 100,000 kilometres on the odometer costs about $0.125 per potential kilometre of use.

$25,000 ÷ 200,000 kilometres (300,000 - 100,000) = $0.125

This isn't a great deal for a nearly new vehicle when you consider a new vehicle is only $0.10 per potential kilometre of use. A better deal would be a cost of $0.08 to $0.10 per potential kilometre of use or about $18,000 to $20,000.

This formula only works if you compare identical makes and features of new and used vehicles.

Because of its relatively young age, a nearly new vehicle will likely have few problems. There may be some repairs down the road, but if and when they happen, don't forget what you paid for the vehicle in the first place. Even if you needed a $500 repair, remember the thousands you saved when you bought the car.

When buying any used car there are things you have to watch out for. We'll discuss them in our next chapter, when we look at cars that are four years old or older.

CHAPTER 60

buying a used car —four years old or older

The used car gets a bad rap. Cars are more reliable today than they were 20 years ago and a good used car can get you around at a fraction of the cost of a new one. Phil Edmonston, author of the Lemon-Aid series of car guides, says, "Canadians are keeping their vehicles about nine years in the west and a little less as you move east. So Canadians are getting a lot more out of their vehicles. With the high cost of new cars, used cars are a great option." One area where the used market has seen excellent results in vehicle longevity is the light truck market. "The light truck market has really exploded in the sense that light trucks are very popular and 50% of light trucks are still on the road after 20 years," says Edmonston. (I guess that explains why I see so many of them around.)

Many people avoid the used car market because when you buy a used car you could end up with a clunker. The older the car and the higher the mileage, the greater the chance you will have problems down the road. However, you'll also have a lower purchase price or lower monthly payments if the car is financed, and generally lower insurance costs because it's an older car. It's the repairs that hurt your wallet, so you want to do your best to make sure the car you are buying is in good condition.

Now that used cars are more reliable you might think this is bad news for car dealers, but Edmonston says that's not so. "Car dealers make much more money selling used cars than they do selling new cars because of the warranty obligations of news cars, servicing obligations, dealing with manufacturers and rebates. Dealers are looking for good used cars as much as possible because the market is shifting in that direction." Some new cars are dropping in price because of rebates and overproduction, and as new models drop in price, it forces used models of that same car to drop in price as well.

The Internet offers more information than ever before when it comes to buying a used car. At www.autotrader.ca, a search option allows you to enter the model you are looking for and the area where you live to see how many models are out there and what they are selling for. You may find there are 168 2002 Honda Civics selling for between $5,400 and $12,800. You can also compare cars for sale with similar mileage and options. It's a great place to start your search.

Car pricing is generally arrived at using car pricing guides known as the "red and black books." These guides are produced for the auto industry and are used by dealers, banks and insurance companies to determine car values. (The blue is *The Kelley Blue Book*, which is sometimes referred to as the black book as well. The red book is *The Canadian Red Book*; more info is available at www.canadianredbook.com.)

Prices vary in the two books. Edmonston says, "The prices are higher in the blue book than generally you will find in the red book. You might want to use the blue book if you're selling a used car and the red book if you are buying one." The books will show the original selling price (MSRP), the wholesale price (what dealers charge other dealers) and the retail price (what dealers charge us). These guides are updated four times a year and can be purchased for about $100, but you can find them for free at a library's reference desk, a credit union or your local bank. If you are on good terms with a dealer, they may even let you have a peek.

You want to do as much research as you can on a model's track record, reliability, repair history and problems specific to that vehicle, such as bad transmissions or faulty power options. Is it likely to be a rust bucket? Will the car be certified and emissions tested? You shouldn't buy a car that isn't unless you are extremely knowledgeable about cars, or you could be hit with huge bills just to get it on the road. You should also take the car to a mechanic for an inspection. For about $100, a good mechanic can tell you what kind of shape the car is in and what repairs it may need down the road. They can also give you an opinion as to what you should be willing to pay for it. If someone won't allow you to take a car to a mechanic, consider it a sign you shouldn't buy it.

Also, take into consideration how far you will be driving the car to help determine its useful life according to your lifestyle. Will it just be a "grocery getter" or will you be racking up kilometres going back and forth to work and on family vacations?

For peace of mind you may want to buy a car with a warranty, but be careful because many offer very limited coverage. Used vehicle warranties from the manufacturer or a reputable dealer may offer some protection, but third-party warranties on small car lots are notorious for being almost worthless and having many loopholes.

Many people are cautious about this approach, even though you can find a good used car privately. Edmonston says, "If people are worried about buying another person's problem, they generally shouldn't be. The problem is not people buying from people, it's people buying from dealers."

If buying privately:

- Ask the previous owner for maintenance records. Is there proof the oil has been changed regularly?

- If a new battery or water pump was installed recently, do they have the paperwork to show it?
- Look for mismatched paint on body panels. Do panels and seams line up perfectly?
- After running the car for a while, park it in an area with dry pavement. Check for oil, transmission or coolant leaks, which are telltale signs of problems ahead.
- Take the car for a long test drive. You would be surprised by how many people don't.

With the overwhelming increase of data accumulation on vehicles, consumers can now arm themselves with more information than ever before. The used vehicle information package, available from most transportation ministries for about $20, can tell you who owned the car and if it has been branded a write-off by an insurance company. While the seller in a private sale is supposed to provide this to you, a dealer doesn't have to. Even if you are buying a car from a dealer, buy the used vehicle information package anyway to see who owned the car.

There are now private companies that track vehicle histories. Edmonston says one such company worth considering is a new one—CarProof in London, Ontario. "I saw what they did when a lady that was thinking of buying a car wanted them to check it. It turned out to be a wreck out of the United States, so she was glad she did," says Edmonston. You can find out more about this service at www.carproof.ca. For about $40, CarProof will verify the car's registration, see if there are liens on the vehicle, determine if it has ever been written off by an insurance company and check its odometer record.

There are also excellent consumer guides that can help you narrow down your search. Edmonston's Lemon-Aid series of car guides is now going into its 35th year. The guides are available in the reference section of every library. For more information, check out www.lemonaidcars.com.

CHAPTER 61

looking out for scams when car buying

Here are a few of the unfortunate things that can happen when you're buying a car.

Curbsiding

I received a call from a young woman who said her mother had worked in a hair salon for 15 years and had been saving up to buy a car. When she finally found one she liked, she bought it with cash. Because she paid cash the bank did not do a lien check on the car and within weeks the vehicle she had saved for for so long was repossessed from her driveway. Why? The man who sold it to her was a con artist. He borrowed money from the bank, bought the car and then sold it to her. When his bank didn't get paid, the car was tracked down to her home and towed away. Sadly, the woman received nothing for the car and returned to her job at the hair salon by bus.

This is known as curbsiding, and if you are considering buying a used car you should know about this practice. Curbsiders are people who sell damaged or stolen cars. Many of these cars have serious flaws and may even have been written off by insurance companies. Curbsiders may tell you they are selling the car for a friend or family member when in fact it's been reconstructed, stolen from the U.S. or had the odometer rolled back.

> Always be sure to check if the vehicle registration number on the paperwork matches the number stamped on the identification plate on the dash of the car.

If a person is selling several cars, but is not a dealer, chances are they are curbsiding vehicles. I have only purchased used vehicles and have found them through dealers and private sales, so I do not wish to discourage anyone from buying used. Just be cautious if someone is trying to close a deal too quickly or does not have the proper paperwork—they could be a curbsider. You could get stuck with a former wreck that's unsafe to drive or a stolen car that could get repossessed from your driveway.

Odometer Fraud

When buying any used car you should take into consideration the possibility of odometer fraud. An odometer can be unhooked and rolled back; with digital odometers a computerized tool can be used to simply type in a new odometer reading.

> As many as 5% to 15% of all used cars may have had their odometers tampered with.

If an odometer is turned back, or unhooked for a while and then reattached, mechanical problems that affect safety could go undetected and unrepaired. You could also face worn-out wheel bearings, tie rod ends and engine parts. Odometer tampering is a crime and driving with a disconnected or inoperable odometer is against the law. On average, most drivers accumulate about 20,000 kilometres annually on their vehicles. If a used car's mileage is substantially lower than this figure, there should be a reasonable explanation why. When shopping for a used car, look for signs that validate the odometer and the car's condition. If buying a car from a dealer, try to contact the previous owner to verify the mileage and shape of the vehicle. If buying privately, ask to see the odometer reading on the contract the owner received when they bought the vehicle. Ask for oil change stickers, request service records, inspect how well doors open and shut and make any other observations you can if you have concerns the odometer may have been tampered with.

So Your New Car Is a Lemon!

Many consumers believe when they buy a brand new vehicle it's guaranteed to be trouble free. Unfortunately there are "lemons" that come off the manufacturing line, with gears that won't shift, sun roofs that leak and brakes that squeal. Many problems are repaired under warranty as they should be, but there is a tightening down on what warranties will cover, so you could have your bumper fall off and find out your "bumper-to-bumper warranty" won't cover it.

The Canadian Motor Vehicle Arbitration Plan, also known as CAMVAP, is an independent agency created in 1994 to resolve disputes between automobile manufacturers and vehicle owners. Best of all, it's free. CAMVAP has handled over 73,000 inquiries from new car buyers and held 4,622 hearings in 446 communities across Canada. More than 70% of all cases in 2003 resulted in an award or settlement favouring the consumer. CAMVAP has ordered 696 vehicles "bought back" by dealerships at a cost of $13.5 million. Another $525,000 was ordered reimbursed to consumers for car repairs.

CAMVAP requires that both parties agree to accept the decision of an impartial arbitrator as binding and final. It can order repairs to a vehicle, a buyback of the vehicle, reimbursement of repair costs, and out-of-pocket expenses up to $500. Your vehicle cannot be more than the current model year plus four years old or have traveled more than 160,000 kilometres. Your car must be for personal use only and cannot be used as a taxi, limousine, hearse, snowplow or for police, fire or municipal services. CAMVAP wants you to try to settle your dispute before it gets involved, but if that doesn't work, call CAMVAP's toll-free hotline at 1-800-207-0685 or check out www.camvap.ca.

CHAPTER 62

asking for
a raise

When people don't deal with their debt or get ahead with their savings, they often start to believe that part of the problem is they just don't make enough money. The broke consumer thinks that if only they had a better salary they would be out of their financial mess. The truth is, someone who hasn't dealt with their overspending ways will never get ahead. If they make $40,000, they will spend $43,000. If they make $60,000, they will spend $65,000. There are high-income earners who make $150,000 a year and spend it all on luxury cars, fine dining and expensive vacations. They are not wealthy and never will be—they are just *living* the high life. The adage "It's not how much you make, it's how much you save" is very true.

This being said, at some point you will want to ask for a raise and should. But there is a right way and a wrong way to go about it.

Barbara Moses, career guru and best-selling author of *What Next? The Complete Guide to Taking Control of Your Working Life*, says that many employees make the mistake of asking for a raise because they are in dire financial straits. Pleading with the boss for more money because the bills are piling up is not only unprofessional, it's also embarrassing. Moses says, "Your needs for a raise are completely irrelevant to your employer. It's how you are contributing to your company and whether you are already being fairly paid that matters."

Instead of telling an employer you need a raise because you are planning a vacation or that you bought a hot tub and your electricity bill is now higher, you need to arm yourself with information that will justify a jump on the pay scale. You have to research and do your homework to make sure you are worthy of a raise before you go and ask for one.

Moses says that first of all, you have to be realistic. "You have to start with an understanding of what your job is worth and secondly what your value is to your employer. Unfortunately, a lot of employees overestimate their value to a company." This is when you have to think about the kind of employee you really are. Are you a go-getter, a company person, a hard worker who gets the job done, who finishes tasks and takes pride in your work? Or are you someone who comes in late, leaves early and muddles along at your job, doing the bare minimum to get by? Are you the complainer, the person with a bad attitude, the person who can't be trusted to get the job done? If you were the boss, would you give yourself a raise?

Bosses, generally speaking, want employees who work hard, unsupervised, who they can trust to do not just a mediocre job but an excellent job. They want employees they don't have to constantly watch, coach or praise. They don't want needy workers. They want people who do their work well so they can get on with the business of being the boss. You should strive to be an ideal employee if you want to get a raise.

The many breaks workers will take throughout the day, whether it is surfing the Internet, running errands or smoking, may be a concern to bosses. As someone who was a smoker briefly when I was younger, I don't like to pick on smokers; I realize it's a difficult habit to quit (but one you should for health reasons as well as financial ones). Still, I am surprised at the sheer number of smoke breaks people in the workplace will take in a given day. Years ago, when employees could smoke on the job or at their desk, perhaps they could get the same amount of work done. However, anyone wanting a cigarette now must leave their workplace, go outside and find a suitable place to light up. It takes about eight minutes to have a cigarette and if we add two minutes to prepare for the smoke break and another two to get back to work after, we are looking at about 12 minutes. It's not uncommon for some smokers to attempt a cigarette break every hour. In an eight-hour work-day that is 96 minutes of smoking breaks. That's a lot of time! That's 480 minutes a week or eight hours—a complete workday! That's about 50 days a year lost to smoking! Now of course other employees take different breaks—breaks for coffee, to surf the Internet or to read the paper. What this calculation shows, however, is that all these breaks really add up. Don't think your boss doesn't keep tabs on who is doing what. Keep all your downtime in mind before you knock on the boss's door to ask for a raise.

According to Moses, the key to getting a raise is to ruthlessly analyze your accomplishments over the past year to identify what you have contributed to your company's bottom line. She says, "Can you say to your boss, this is what I have done this year that has generated the company a significant amount of income?"

She says you should also look at your workload and determine if your job function has changed. "You may be described as an assistant manager when in fact you are doing manager-level work. Maybe your duties have changed but your job title has not. This can be a strategy to show your boss that you are deserving of a raise."

Another plan of action that can work for you is to simply go to your boss and say, "I want a 10% raise and I want to know what the best way is to get it." Being aggressive can show that you have drive and want to get ahead within your company.

This approach brings to mind the conversation between Tom Cruise and Cuba Gooding Jr. in the movie *Jerry Maguire*. If you recall, Cruise had to shout, "Show me the money!" to satisfy his football star client. But he started out by saying, "Help me, help you." This is the message you want to give your superiors. By telling your boss *help me, help you*, you are really saying you want to demonstrate that you are worthy of a 10% raise.

When you take this approach a couple of things can happen. "The boss might say, 'Here is what you need to do to get a raise.' Or the boss might say, 'I just don't have that 10% discretionary control' and it may be very true that he or she does not," explains Moses. It's good to find out just who has the authority to grant you a raise and there is certainly no harm in asking. In fact, putting the cards on the table can help you find out who is in charge of the company purse strings so you'll know who it is that can approve a pay increase.

Check job boards like www.monster.ca to see if similar jobs are available and how much they pay. Doing so gives you leverage in negotiating for a raise. Remember, knowledge is power.

Moses says that depending on the company you work for there may be limits as to what they will pay even though a similar company may pay more. "Companies have salary scales. Depending on the company, they may decide they want to be in the industry's top 10% or top 30% or even the bottom 10%. In other words, you should understand that if you are a director of research and development in one type of organization you might be able to earn a greater salary in another organization because of how their pay structure works." It will also depend on the kind of job you have. I know someone who owns a trucking company and the salaries paid are determined on mathematical equations based on mileage, distance, weight and time. These factors will dictate the salary of the worker and no amount of charm and persuasion will change the math.

Moses adds that "You are of much greater value if you are working in a sector where keeping people happy is very important.

For example, the pharmaceutical industry tends to pay people very well and tries hard to keep their employees happy. Most of the workers are very well educated and therefore very expensive to replace." By contrast, if you are working in a sector where education and jobs skill levels are not as high, then you will be easier to replace and have less bargaining power because there is a bigger pool to draw from to replace you.

However, if you are truly deserving of a raise, it's in your current company's best interests to keep you happy by granting you a pay hike. If they don't, in a hot job market, you can vote with your feet and go elsewhere for another job with better pay and benefits. If you ask for a raise and don't get it, but decide to stay with the company, you have still let your employer know where you stand. Good employers will respect you for asking and will keep you in mind when preparing future budgets.

CHAPTER 63

changing careers

.

Years ago, people chose one career and stuck with it, but chances are you will switch careers two, three or four times in your working life. People are living longer and you may wish to try something new when you reach 50; after all, you may still be working another 20 years. You may also decide to work for yourself and open your own business, which has its own risks and rewards. If you are in a job that is no longer desirable or is not paying you as much as you feel you deserve, you should look at your options. If you want to stay in good financial shape and make sure your bank book doesn't take a hit if you decide to chart a new course, you will want to make sure you manage your career choices wisely.

Career guru Barbara Moses says that changes in the work-place have transformed the way we should think about our jobs. It's imperative to be a "career activist" and take charge of your career choices. Moses says, "You should always keep your job skills up to date so that you can always find someone else to sell them to. You don't necessarily have to have an employer waiting in the wings to hire you, but you should ensure that if you needed to or wanted to, you could sell your skills to someone else." You may be content in your current position but at any time you could be the victim of a new boss, downsizing or restructuring. Moses says you have to be ready to jump ship if the time comes. "What you want to say from an individual's point of view is that you are ready to jump ship if you had to, because if you can't jump ship then you don't have choices." Keeping your skills up to date may mean upgrading your education and following the latest trends and shifts in your industry.

Often when people think about changing careers they think of it as a radical move, but it doesn't have to be. You can make a transition from one career to another without it causing major upheaval in your life. "People can retool their career at any time, but there are different ways of doing it," says Moses. "A lot of people think the only choice is to make a grand career change, which is usually very expensive because it often involves going back to school. If you do this, typically your great experience in your former profession will not be recognized, so essentially you are starting out all over again."

It makes far better sense to reconfigure your skills. For example, a police officer could become a security expert or a teacher could become a trainer. This allows an easier transition than a machinist becoming a florist. Constantly thinking about your career and making sure you are in a position to jump ship if you had to will also lessen some of the stress and anxieties of worrying what could happen if you did lose your job. It will help you regain personal power and confidence and allow you to feel that you have options and something to offer not just one company but several.

If you are considering changing careers, you may be tempted by the latest hot prospects on job boards or trends in the newspaper. Moses says to be careful before committing to a new direction in your life based on careers that seem hot at the time. "I never believe that anyone should make a career choice based on what jobs are hot and what's not. What's hot tomorrow could be rendered obsolete six months down the road because of changes in government, new technology, labour shortages, immigration or policy changes. That's not the right way to plan your career. You should plan your career based on what you want to do and what you are good at. Forget the hot jobs."

For more information on Moses, check out her website, www.bmoses.com.

Since this book is about getting out of debt and building wealth, I also asked Moses about her own personal experiences with debt and money management. She agrees that many people are overspending and digging themselves into debt for all the wrong reasons. "People can be owned by stuff and then they have to buy more stuff to complement the stuff they already have."

She says her father gave her some interesting advice when she was getting married. Her dad told her, "Mom may put pressure on you to get silver. Then when you have silver, you are going to want china. Then when you have china, you are going to need a place to display that china. Then one day you are going to get up and you will see all this stuff around you that doesn't add any value to your life."

Moses advises, "Know what is really important to you and never make a purchase without taking it through a sieve of how [this will] add pleasure to your life. Many people use money as a placeholder to satisfy all kinds of other things. When people feel good about their lives, money is less important." It's something Moses also refers to as "decrapifying"—getting rid of the crap in your life that does not have true meaning. She says, "Evaluate your successes and what you have not against others, but by your own internal standard, and be happy with what you have, rather than what you don't have."

I think your father would be proud, Barbara.

---

CHAPTER 64

giving to charity

Having all the money in the world will not make you a happy individual. It's often said, "You can't take it with you" and you can't. That's why once you get a handle on wasteful spending and have your financial situation under control you may want to consider giving back to the community in some way. It could be your local hospital, church or school. You might decide to donate to the food bank on a regular basis or sponsor a child in a third-world country. When you do it, you realize that it truly is better to give than to receive.

For years my wife wanted our family to sponsor a child in Africa. "If we all do our part ..." she would say. I always felt our money was better off in a mutual fund or paying the next bill that came through the door. While it is important to get your financial house in order, there will come a time when your good habits will have saved you money that you can use to help others. Think about this: If you have a credit card bill of $2,000 with an annual interest rate of 18%, you are giving $30 a month or $360 a year in interest charges to some huge, faceless corporation. Imagine if that credit card was paid off one day and you instead gave that $30 a month to sponsor a child stuck in poverty. You could help a child in a dire situation enjoy a better life, go to school and get medicare.

We sponsor a child in Zimbabwe through World Vision Canada. His name is Sibanda Nkosiyapha and he is 10 years old. This little boy has AIDS. We give $40 a month, a little more than the usual $35, so World Vision can buy extra drugs to help him lead a normal life. It is a joy to get a letter from him once in a while or a photo to see how he is doing. (He is the son I never had!)

I was fortunate enough to travel to Africa with World Vision in the fall of 2004. I went to Gulu, Uganda, and was shocked at the conditions that people continue to live in. I saw entire families live in homes no larger than what Canadians might have for a garden shed. For me the trip was a huge eye-opener to the poverty that still exists in the world and also a reminder of the wonderful life we are able to enjoy in Canada.

Since this is a book about saving money, keep in mind that for any charitable donation you make, you'll be issued a tax receipt, so you could get 20% to 40% of your donation back at tax time! This is just one more reason to consider charitable contributions when your financial picture improves.

Summary of factors affecting your score

The FICO score is calculated based on the information contained in your Equifax credit history. While knowing your actual score is a good start, understanding the key factors affecting your FICO score is much more important. These factors will provide you direction on how you can increase or maintain your FICO score over time.

The negative factors listed below are reasons why your FICO score is not higher. Your focus on these factors will help you to raise your FICO score over time. These negative factors are provided in order of impact to your score, the first factor listed indicates where you stand to gain the most points over time and so on.

You have recently been seeking credit as reflected by the number of inquiries posted on your credit file in the last 12 months
Research shows that consumers who are seeking new credit accounts are riskier than consumers who are not seeking credit. Inquiries are the only information lenders have that indicates a consumer is actively seeking credit. There are different types of inquiries that reside on your credit bureau report. The score only considers those inquiries that were posted as a result of you applying for credit. Other types of inquiries, such as account review inquiries (where a lender with whom you have

an account has received your credit report) or consumer disclosure inquiries (where you have requested a copy of your own report) are not considered by the score. The scores can identify "rate shopping" so that one credit search leading to multiple inquiries being reported is usually only counted as a single inquiry. For most consumers, the presence of a few inquiries on your credit file has a limited impact on FICO scores. A common misperception is that every single inquiry will drop your score a certain number of points. This is not true. The impact of inquiries on your score will vary—depending on your overall credit profile. Inquiries will usually have a larger impact on the score for consumers with limited credit history and on consumers with previous late payments. The most prudent action to raise your score over time is to apply for credit only when you need it.

As time passes the age of your most recent inquiry will increase and your score will rise as a result, provided you do not apply for additional credit in the meantime. Our best recommendation—apply for credit only when you need it.

The length of time your revolving or non-revolving accounts have been established is too short

This reason is based on the age of the revolving or non-revolving charge accounts on your credit bureau report (the age of your oldest revolving or non-revolving charge account, the average age of your revolving or non-revolving charge accounts, or both). A revolving account such as Visa, MasterCard, or retail store card allows consumers to make a minimum monthly payment and roll or "revolve" the remainder of their balance to the next month. Non-revolving accounts such as American Express and Diners Club must be paid off in full each month. Research shows that consumers with longer credit histories have better repayment risk than those with shorter credit histories. Also, consumers who frequently open new accounts have greater repayment risk than those who do not.

It is a good idea to only apply for credit when you really need it. Meanwhile, maintain low-to-moderate balances and be sure to make your payments on time. Your score should improve as your revolving credit history ages.

The amount owed on your non-mortgage related accounts is too high

The score measures how much you owe on the non-mortgage related accounts (revolving, non-revolving, and installment) that are listed on your credit bureau report. Research reveals that consumers owing larger amounts on their credit accounts have greater future repayment risk than those who owe less. (For credit cards, the total outstanding balance on your last statement is generally the amount that will show in your credit bureau report. Note that even if you pay off your credit cards in full each and every month, your credit bureau report may show the last billing statement balance on those accounts.)

Paying off your debts and maintaining low balances will help to improve your credit score. Consolidating or moving your debt around from one account to another will usually not, however, raise your score, since the same amount is still owed.

Proportion of loan balances to original loan amounts is too high

Simply having installment loans and owing money on them does not mean you are a high-risk borrower. To the contrary, paying down installment loans is a good sign that you are able and willing to manage and repay debt, and evidence of successful repayment weighs favorably on your credit rating. The FICO score examines many aspects of your current installment loan and revolving balances. One measurement is to compare outstanding installment balances against the original loan amounts. Generally, the closer the loans are to being fully paid off, the better the score. Compared to other measurements of indebtedness, however, this has limited influence on the FICO score.

Paying down installment loans on a timely basis generally reflects well on your credit score. But if you want to improve your score, one way to do it is to try to pay the loans, (especially non-mortgage installment loans) down as quickly as you can.

Document courtesy of Equifax Canada.

Index

A

accelerated payments (mortgage), 189–190
accidents (auto), 114
ACORN, 87–88
"acts of God," 212
alcohol, 60
American credit companies, 71
amortization, 187, 188–189
annuity, 175
appraisals
    home, 226
    and home/tenant insurance, 212
asset classes, 160
Association of Community Organizations for Reform Now, 87–88
At the Crease, 10

B

baby boomers, 155–156, 169
Bach, David, 60
backyard (selling home), 225
bad debt *v.* good debt, 64–66
Badgley, Timothy, 223
"bait and switch" tactics, 242–243
bank account, monthly review, 55
Bank of Canada, 102
bankruptcy, 79, 81, 89–95
bankruptcy trustee, 92, 93
bar codes, 134
basement
    apartments, 205
    renovations, 217
bathroom renovations, 215–216
beater (car), 236
Bill C-55, 93
biweekly payments (mortgage), 189–190
black book (cars), 254
"blend-and-extend" (mortgage), 197
blue book (cars), 254

borrowing to invest, 65
borrow short, invest long, 39
brand name foods, 128, 129
breaking a mortgage, 194–197
Bre-X, 161
Brockelsby, Gerry, 159
budget worksheet, 44–46
Buell, Stan, 146–148
bulk foods, 129
"bumper-to-bumper" warranty, 259
"buy-and-hold stock market," 162

C

calculators for 0% financing, 243
Campbell, Laurie, 53–56, 70–72
CAMVAP, 259–260
Canada Education Savings Grant, 178
Canadian Bankers Association, 178
Canadian Bar Association, 152
Canadian Consumer Alert, 2
Canadian Life and Health Insurance Association, 120, 121
Canadian Loss Experience Automobile Rating (CLEAR), 112
Canadian Motor Vehicle Arbitration Plan, 259–260
Canadian Payday Loan Association, 87, 88
Canadian Red Book, 254
capital appreciation (real estate), 203
capital gains tax, 200
career change, 266–268
car insurance, 108–116
car loans, 97
CarProof, 256
cars
    buying new, 236–239
    and cash incentives, 240–241
    depreciation, 239
    financing, 239
    leasing, 244–249
    options and accessories, 237
    pricing, 237–238